Microeconomic Studies

Edited by W. Güth, J. McMillan and H.-W. Sinn

Bernd Gutting

Taxation, Housing Markets, and the Markets for Building Land

An Intertemporal Analysis

With 14 Figures

Springer-Verlag
Berlin Heidelberg New York
London Paris Tokyo

Dr. rer. pol. Bernd Gutting
Fakultät für VWL und Statistik
Universität Mannheim
A5, A, D-6800 Mannheim

ISBN-13: 978-3-642-45632-9 e-ISBN-13: 978-3-642-45630-5
DOI: 10.1007/978-3-642-45630-5

Softcover reprint of the hardcover 1st edition 1987

2142/3140-543210

Preface

Almost everywhere in the world housing policies play an important role in government programs. Especially in the industrialized Western economies housing policy issues are triggered mainly by two developments:

- growing population density and increasing environmental pollution enforce a systematic planning of regional and urban development;
- all social groups want to participate in the increasing welfare of the domestic economies; until today housing policy is considered an appropriate tool for redistribution and social policy.

Taxation serves as an important instrument for the realization of the political objectives mentioned above. Surprisingly, there exists wide-spread consent (even on the academic side) on the effectivity of this instrument. However, strictly speaking this consent concerns only the short run. Long-term effects are usually ignored. Therefore, there is always the inherent risk in these policies that (supposed) market inefficiencies will not be cured, but merely carried forward, and possibly amplified.

Moreover, it is characteristic for the political discussion that there is no consistent notion of what efficient housing and land markets ought to look like. Generally accepted for example, is the position that land speculation should be fought whereever possible. Hardly anyone asks the question whether the holding of building land will be beneficial to the economy as a whole, and not only to the speculant.

This book gives such and related questions careful attention. And although the theoretical framework used in this book only provides a very simplistic image of the reality, the results to be derived in the succeeding chapters should give reason for thinking over some of the well-loved notions about the workings of housing and land markets.

The list of those to whom I am indebted is a long one. Especially my teachers at the University of Mannheim, Hans Heinrich Nachtkamp and Hans Werner Sinn, stimulated my interest in economics, and in the particular subject of this book. I am also grateful for many helpful comments from Richard Arnott, Scott Freeman, Paul Hobson, Peter Howitt, John McMillan, David Pines and John Whalley. And thanks to Helga Häusler for an excellent typing job.

Munich, June 1987

Contents

I. Introduction

1. MOTIVATION

A central purpose of economics is to describe and develop mechanisms which allocate the scarce resources of an economy to the production of goods and services in a way that makes the individuals in that economy as well off as possible. In mixed economies, resource allocation decisions are taken by the private and the public sector.

In the succeeding chapters issues of market failure are neglected. The only activity of the public sector consists in the execution of a transfer program. In order to undertake such expenditures the government must acquire resources. Since our main concern is with the resource allocation effects of public sector activity rather than with more aggregative issues, we will not consider questions related to public debt or the creation of new money but concentrate on tax policies.

Allocation problems arising from the imposition of different sorts of taxation are well known. In diverting resources to the public sector these taxes may distort the workings of the market economy to varying degrees by inducing market agents to make economic decisions different from those they would have made in a tax-free economy. It is a goal of this book to describe such tax-induced distortions for two particular markets - the markets for housing services and the market for building land.

In that, the analysis of chapters II and III is a positive one: it tries to explain how various taxes affect the decisions of individual agents. But the analysis also is a normative one: it tries to evaluate various forms of taxation from a social point of view. The Pareto criterion is the measure that allows us to evaluate the economic performance of a certain tax (system). If one accepts the notion that a competitive equilibrium satisfies the requirements of Pareto optimality, all tax induced distortions of this equilibrium must be associated with deadweight losses. It is another goal of this book to develop forms of taxation which either cause no deadweight losses, i.e. which are <u>neutral</u>, or at least reduce deadweight losses incurred in existing tax systems.

Analysis of the taxation of housing and land is neither new nor rare. On the other hand the theoretical frameworks used to examine the effects of taxation are very often static ones. And where dynamic frameworks are chosen [for example in Feldstein (1977) or Calvo et al. (1979)], land can be used for production purposes only. The model used in this book is dynamic and considers explicitly that land may also be used as an asset.

The results derived in chapter III differ in many ways from these which determine today's prevailing opinions about tax effects. Moreover, the model allows, rudimentarily, for an examination of the interdependency of financing and investment decisions. This extension of traditional analysis also provides deeper insights, particularly into the incidence of current income tax laws.

The following section contains a brief description of the model's institutional framework.

2. A GENERAL FRAMEWORK WITH HOUSING AND VACANT LAND MARKETS

Subject of the subsequent analysis are economic functions involved in the run of events in housing and land markets. Figure 1 features these functions as well as the relationships between them. Six functions are distinguished.
These are carried out by

- construction firms (this term represents all productive sectors in the economy exclusive of the housing and financial sectors),
- housing investors (or landlords),
- households,
- landowners,
- financial institutions,
- the public sector.

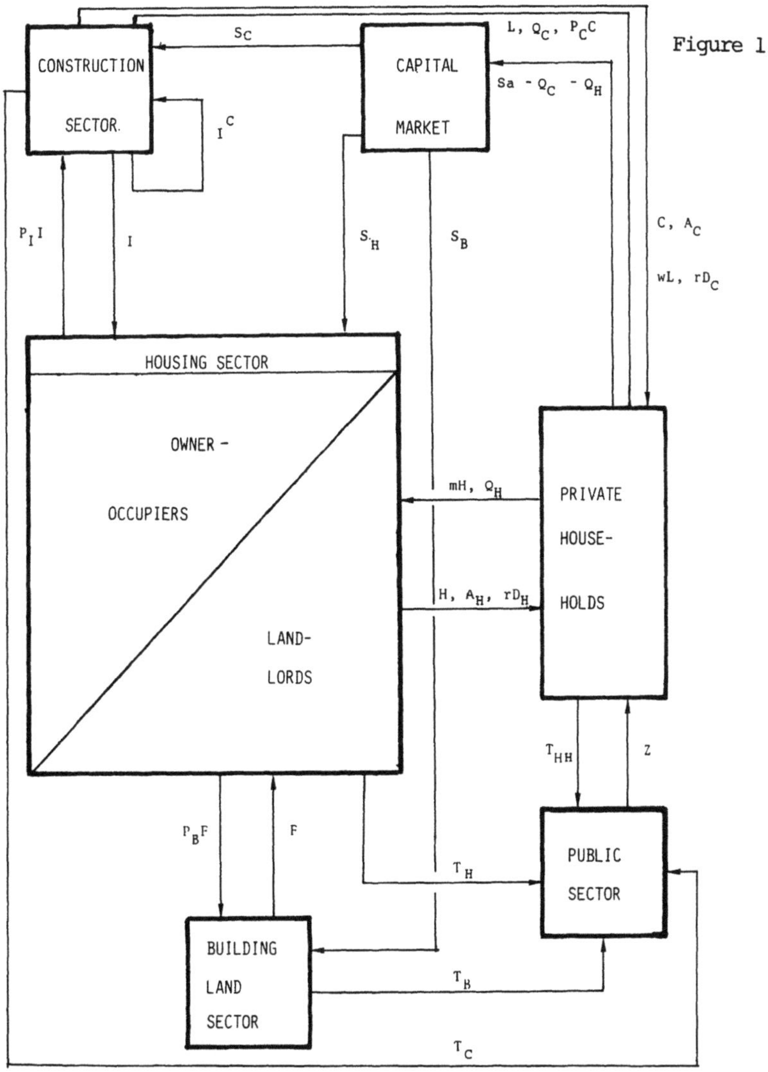

Figure 1

The construction firms erect and maintain housing units by order and for account of housing investors (in the following referred to as landlords). The landlords purchase these construction services, I, at a per unit price P_I. The flow variable I covers the building material as well as the human labor necessary for housing construction. The construction of <u>new</u> housing units requires, besides construction services, land. This can be acquired at a per unit price P_B from landowners. In figure 1 the parameter F denotes the flow of land consumed for building purposes in a given period. One consequence of the functional approach is that building land will be built upon immediately after its acquisition.

The newly constructed rental accomodation ceteris paribus increases the existing stock of housing units, H. Each housing unit is assumed to produce exactly one unit of housing services per period. The parameter H therefore also measures the supply of housing services in a given period. Housing services are sold at a per-unit price m to private households. In addition to housing services these households consume another consumption good, C, provided by the construction firms at a price of P_C per unit. The good C as well as construction services are produced from capital and labor, L. The parameter w denotes the going wage rate.

The description of the model's financial sphere is based on the observation that every enterprise is actually owned by private households. Because of this households receive firm profits. The parameter A symbolizes these profit shares (the subindexes H and C indicate whether these flows come from the housing or the construction sector). On the other hand households apply a part of their savings, Sa, to increase the equity terms of their enterprises. The parameters Q_H and Q_C denote those fractions of private savings which flow back to firms in form of equity. The remainder of private savings is offered on the capital market, where financial intermediaries arrange credit contracts between households and firms. For the sake of simplicity it is assumed that the property rights to a unit of building land do not change until it is sold to a potential landlord. Therefore there is no demand for credit by landowners.

Thus, the amount $Sa - Q_H - Q_C$ is invested in private bonds; as a result, in a given period the stocks of obligations in the construction sector, D_C, and in the housing sector, D_H, increase by S_C or S_H, respectively.

In every period both sectors must serve their outstanding debt according to the going interest rate, r. Consequently, in addition to their labor income, w L, and dividend payments, $A_H + A_C$, households receive interest payments by the amount of $r(D_H + D_C)$ in any given period.

A complete description of the households' income also requires the consideration of transfer payments, Z, coming from the public sector. In order to finance these payments, the government imposes and collects taxes in the construction sector (T_C), the housing sector (T_H), the land sector (T_B), and the sector of private households (T_{HH}).

In chapter III we will confront the tax policy with the requirement that it must not prevent the economy outlined in figure I from reaching its welfare optimum. In order to show whether current tax policies meet this requirement we have to know what the welfare optimum looks like.

The second theorem of welfare economics* states that the general equilibrium of a perfectly competitive laissez-faire economy also represents a welfare optimum since it satisfies the conditions of Pareto-optimality. Knowing this, the general equilibrium conditions can be applied to evaluate the effects of particular taxes or entire tax systems.

At first glance it seems hard, if not impossible, to derive equilibrium conditions in the context of the model economy sketched in figure 1. Not less than four intertemporal decision problems have to be solved simultaneously. However, we can by-pass these problems by referring to Fisher's separation theorem.**

This theorem states that when all agents have perfect foresight, the output decisions of firms and the consumption and labor-supply decisions of households can be analyzed independently from each other. As is shown in Hirshleifer***, Robinson Crusoe's production plan is independent of his preference system. The utility maximizing consumption plan only requires that Robinson's opportunity set is also maximized, given resource endowments and technology. The latter in turn implies that the market value (or capital value) of Robinson's enterprise is at its maximum.

---

*See Lange (1942); the formal proof of this theorem is provided by Arrow (1951); Malinvaud (1953) proved the existence of the intertemporal equilibrium generally for a decision problem with infinite planning horizon; see also Dorfman, Samuelson and Solow (1958), in particular pp. 310.

**See Fisher (1931), Hirshleifer (1970).

***See Hirshleifer (1970).

We will utilize the separation theorem for our analysis. In what follows, a partial equilibrium analysis will be carried out, focusing on housing and (building) land markets without loosing track of the relations between these two sectors and the remaining components of the economy in figure 1. It is assumed that the behavior of landlords and landowners can be approximated by the behaviour of representative agents. Both, the representative landlord and the representative landowner are assumed to have an infinite planning horizon as well as perfect foresight, to behave as perfect competitors, and to act rationally.

The decisions of the representative agents are the results of individual optimization problems. As a consequence of the functional approach used in this book, landlord and landowner act solely in the interest of private households. Therefore every decision they make has to aim at the maximization of the households' opportunity sets. The separation theorem tells us how the landlord has to plan his housing investment and how the landowner has to adjust his land supply over time in order to meet this requirement: the plans of both agents are optimal if (and only if) the resulting market values of their enterprises are maximized.

Both agents make their decisions independently of each other. The individual plans are coordinated by market mechanisms. Although prices are taken as given as far as the individual decision problems are concerned, they are endogenous, i.e. the results of the clearing of markets. In addition, since both agents are endowed with perfect foresight, there is no need for both of them to revise any decision taken in the past.

3. SUMMARY OF RESULTS

The tax regulations discussed in chapter III are fundamental inasmuchas they describe the biggest common denominator of the tax laws currently in force in most of the industrialized Western economies - at least as far as the taxation of housing and building land sectors is concerned. The analysis also deals with suggestions advanced in the recent tax literature on how to amend current tax laws in order to meet the requirements of efficiency.

The prevailing opinion concerning the taxation of land is strongly influenced by Ricardo's notion of the impacts of a tax on pure land rent. According to Ricardo such a tax has no influence on the relative profitability of land in different uses, i.e. is neutral [Ricardo (1951)]. One of the first to challenge this view was Feldstein [Feldstein (1977)]. By introducing land as a third factor of production into a traditional overlapping-generations model, Feldstein showed that Ricardo's central assumption about the elasticity of supply of non-land factors of production might be a weak one. Taking capital accumulation processes into account, Feldstein's analysis yields the result that the introduction of a tax on the pure rent of land induces an intensification of the accumulation of capital and thus leads to a higher capital-labor ratio and to a lower net yield on capital and a higher wage rate. But Feldstein's results as well depend on one crucial assumption: the decision-maker's extreme disinterest in the well-being of his descendants. By applying Barro's modification of overlapping-generation models [Barro (1974)], Ricardo's neutrality theorem can be restated. Because the agents' planning horizon now is an infinite one, they anticipate that the present value of tax-induced additional future transfer payments equals their current tax-liabilities [Calvo, Kotlikoff, Rodriguez (1979)]. Therefore, in this world, there is no tax-induced incentive for the decision-makers to change their before-tax consumption-savings decision; the tax is fully capitalized in the price of land. It follows straightforwardly that these results also describe the impact of a tax on the value of land, value defined as the present value of future rents.

However, the neutrality results derived from traditional general equilibrium models of the type mentioned above seem to be predetermined by the chosen model structure. In particular decisive seems the fact that in general there is only one use of land - land as a factor of production - and that land is fully employed at every point of time. Because of the assumed non-existence of vacant land the rational landowner is deprived at the start of any opportunity to react to the capital owner's attempt to shift the burden of the tax. Chapter III shows that the landowner's reactions to the imposition of a tax on land rent (land value) are very pronounced if an alternative use of land - land as an asset - is introduced into a framework with perfect foresight and infinite planning horizons.

The economic intuition for these reactions is easy to provide. Let us first consider the incidence of a tax on the rent or the value, respectively, of vacant land. In a world without taxation the equilibrium time-path of land supply is the one that generates a return on the remaining stock of vacant land equal to the return on other assets; the per-unit price of vacant land has to grow at a rate equal to the market interest rate [Hotelling (1931)]. If a tax is levied on the rent (the value) of vacant land, there is an incentive for the landowner to substitute tax-free assets for the taxed one. The initial effect of the introduction of the tax therefore will be an increase in the supply of vacant land which in turn, given the demand for vacant land, causes a drop in the costs of building land. These initial distortions also affect the future development of the vacant land market. The immediate response to the introduction of the tax causes a reduction in the supply of building land in future periods. Given the time path of demand this must result in an increase of the land price's growth rate. As a matter of fact the new equilibrium requires that the increase in the price of land is sufficient to cover the increased opportunity cost of holding vacant land, i.e. interest foregone plus tax liabilities.

But not only that the tax induces the landowner to alter his plans, the landlord also deviates from his laissez-faire investement plans when vacant land is taxed. The initial decrease in the costs of building land has two effects: first, it induces the landlord to choose a lower capital intensity for new rental accomodation, second, because overall investment cost are also lower than in the tax-free world, it calls forth an intensification of new housing investment. Moreover, because the landlord anticipates that the landowner will succeed in partially shifting his tax burden in the long run in the form of faster rising land prices, his propensity to invest increases at a lower rate after the tax is imposed. This in turn causes an acceleration in both the growth of the rental rate and the house price. Obviously the tax on vacant land is not neutral inasmuchas it helps the housing sector to a "short-term" construction boom and generally discriminates against the asset "real estate" in the long run.

However, the short-term impacts of land taxation are less clear-cut if one takes into account that the landlord's stock of housing units is also subject to taxation. If the market value (rent) of the whole housing stock represents the tax base, the tax reduces the rentability of investment in new rental accomodation and thus works against the short-term impacts of a tax on vacant land. If the market value (rent) of only the land included in the stock of housing units is subject to taxation - in the recent tax literature such a tax is referred to as "site value" tax - the tax induced discrimination of housing investment is less distinct; compared to the previous tax arrangement the "site value" tax results in a government subsidy on the use of non-land factors of production, affecting the capital intensity at which building takes place as well as the volume of new housing investment.

Facing these results, one has to wonder whether there is any method of taxing land that does not affect the landowner's or the landlord's decision problems. Apparently the landowner can always dodge the tax burden by selling the taxed item and buying tax-free assets with the released equity. For this reason the analysis of a tax which covers all interest bearing assets suggests itself. Provided that the tax rate assessed on the current market values is the same for all assets, it turns out that at least in our partial equilibrium framework such a "comprehensive" property tax is neutral. Neither for the landlord nor for the landowner is there an incentive to respond to the imposition of the tax by changing their original plans. Both realize that, although they could reduce the present value of land tax liability by altering investment and sale plans, the present value of the property tax as a whole would remain unchanged. Taxes have to be paid on land as well as on other assets that could be purchased by foregoing housing investment or advancing the sale of vacant land.

However, since the results stated above are derived by applying partial equilibrium analysis, they have to be handled with care. First, a (comprehensive) property tax can be levied only on assessable assets. Human capital would still be tax exempt. Resulting distortions will be amplified by tax-induced changes in the households' consumption-savings decisions. A general property tax lowers the opportunity cost of todays consumption, thus hampering the capital accumulation process in an economy [Sinn (1985b), Nachtkamp (1986)] .

Another perceivable alternative concerning the taxation of developed as well as vacant land could consist in the imposition of a tax on land area independent of its value. It will be shown that such a "per-unit" land tax is neutral. The reason for this neutrality is that the landlord succeeds in shifting back his entire tax burden to the landowner, who in turn does not consider the alteration of sale plans as a rational response. He realizes that advancing land sales would not result in a reduction of his tax burden; because of the properties of the tax base and the landlord's reaction to the tax the present value of the landowners' tax payments is independent of when vacant land is sold. The only result would be a decline of "before-tax" sale revenues since the new time path of land supply would necessarily deviate from the revenue-maximizing laissez-faire path. The landowner's optimal strategy therefore is to maintain his initially chosen intertemporal supply plan, reconciling himself to the burden of the tax.

Related to the inefficiencies arising from current property tax regulations are those caused by the present tax treatment of income from real estate. Similar to the results of the property tax analysis and in accordance with the established income tax literature [see for example Schanz (1886), Haig (1921), Simons (1938), Johannson (1961), Canada (1966), Sinn (1985b)] a comprehensive income tax is neutral (as long as we stay within the partial equilibrium context specified above). Since in equilibrium every asset yields the same rate of return, and since all these incomes are taxed uniformly, there is no loophole that allows for tax avoidance. Consequently, the landlord's and landowner's optimal strategies consist of maintaining their laissez-faire plans.

A comprehensive taxation of income from real estate would require that

- the landowner has to pay taxes on capital gains at the time they accrue, and
- that the landlord's income tax base is defined as rental revenues plus accrued capital gains minus capital losses caused by deterioration minus mortgage interest.

Even a casual glance on current income tax laws will reveal that the above requirements are not in the least met. In particular the treatment of capital gains is far from being satisfying. In all developed Western economies capital gains are virtually tax exempt. Nowhere are accrued capital gains subject to taxation, and where a tax on realized capital gains is levied, the tax is effective only if these gains exceed a (typically large) allowance.

Although most economists working on the subject agree that the tax exemption of capital gains is detrimental from an efficiency point of view, they are sceptical about suggestions on how to cure this undesirable situation. The taxation of accrued capital gains is usually rejected with a reference to administrative obstacles. Provisos against the taxation of realized capital gains are based on the (prevailing) opinion that this would induce the landowner to postpone the sale of his asset since he now will spot an opportunity to reduce the present value of his tax payments [see for example David (1968), Feldstein und Yitzhaki (1978), Boadway and Kitchen (1984)].

Chapter III provides the formal proof that this popular view is not valid in general. To see why, consider a landowner who has to decide whether to sell a given area of vacant land today or tomorrow. In a general equilibrium context he will be indifferent between both alternatives. This results because, according to the Hotelling-rule, vacant land yields the same return as alternative investments. The landowner would remain indifferent between the two choices if a tax were levied on the value of vacant land at the time it is sold: since the tax base grows at a rate that is equal to the rate of discount, the present value of tax payments is independent of when the sale takes place. A tax on realized capital gains differs from this sales tax inasmuchas the former is assessed only on capital gains accumulated between a certain base-period and the date of sale, leaving the base-period price tax-free. Therefore, the tax on realized capital gains can be interpreted as a combination of a (neutral) sales tax and a government subsidy on the sale of vacant land. Since the <u>current</u> value of the governmental subsidy is constant over time, its <u>present</u> value is bigger the earlier the sale takes place. These reflections allow for the conclusion that, provided the asset yields no intermediate benefits, there is no "lock-in" effect incurred in the taxation of realized capital gains. On the contrary, the tax induces an unambigeous incentive to advance the sale of the asset. In the general case where the asset "vacant land" yields intermediate benefits, the occurrance of a "lock-in" effect depends on the relative share of these benefits in the gross rate of return.

However, the intuitive example given above does not explain the impact of a tax on realized capital gains completely. Subject to taxation are capital gains realized in the flow of vacant land sold in a given period; the capital gains accrued in the stock of vacant land in the same period are still tax exempt. The latter implies that vacant land in so far is more desirable relative to other taxable assets. The preferential treatment provides a definite incentive to postpone the sale of vacant land. It can be shown that on balance the latter impact predominates, i.e. that current income tax laws cause a deferral of land development. But it has to be stressed that this arises because of the exclusion of accrued capital gains from the tax base rather than from a taxation of realized capital gains per se.

Another controversial issue in the political discussion on taxation is the income tax treatment of owner-occupants. Computed rental incomes from owner-occupation are in general tax exempt. With the exception of the U.S. this tax exemption also implies that mortgage interest payments are not deductible. The tax exemption usually is defended with allusion to redistributive goals. It will be shown in chapter III that this rationalization is invalid. At least those who are serious about the redistribution argument fail to notice two important points: the influence of the non-deductibility of interest payments on financing preferences and the interdependency between financing and investment decisions. Quite obviously the tax exemption of imputed rental income provides a loophole for income tax avoidance - provided the landlord is able to finance with equity. The reason for the tax-induced preference for equity financing is the cost associated with this alternative: compared to the costs of debt financing, which are proportionate to the gross market interest rate, the opportunity cost of equity financing, i.e. interest foregone (which is proportionate to the market interest rate net of tax), are lower.

From this it follows straightforwardly that present income tax laws discriminate against the "poor" landlord, who cannot dispose of sufficient equity in order to finance his housing investment in the cheapest way. Only in the U.S., where owner-occupiers are allowed to deduct mortgage interest payments from other income, does this discrimination not occcur (however, households without any taxable income are discriminated against in the U.S. as anywhere else).

Whether the above tax regulations can be criticized under efficiency considerations as well is less clear-cut. They doubtlessly cause welfare losses to the extent that they violate the conditions for an intersectoral efficient allocation of the various factors of production needed to construct rental accomodation. On the other hand, the tax exemption of imputed rental income unambigeously represents a Pareto improvement if intertemporal distortions caused by a comprehensive income tax are taken into account. It is well known from the literature on the subject [for example Meade Committee (1978), Sinn (1985)], that the taxation of interest income, an important component of a comprehensive income tax system,drives a wedge between the value of the net marginal product of capital stock and the households' rate of time preference. Compared to a Pareto-optimal equilibrium the households' propensity to save is insufficient, since the opportunity cost of dissaving decrease due to taxation. It is shown in chapter III that as a consequence of the tax exemption of imputed rental income the laissez-faire equality of the net marginal value product and the rate of time preference may be reestablished in the sector of owner-occupied housing.

Chapter III also contains a proposal how the tax treatment of not-imputed rental income could be modified in order to meet the requirements of intertemporal efficiency. The basic idea for this proposal is provided in Sinn (1985). It is shown that, if current income tax laws were amended to the extent that prevailing periodical depreciation allowances are replaced by the permission to immediately deduct <u>all</u> expenses related to housing investment (i.e. expenses for maintenance, construction services, <u>and</u> building land), the net marginal value product of the entire housing stock would be equal to the rate of time preference.

In addition to these more global aspects of the taxation of housing and building land sectors the analysis of chapter III also focuses on more detailed issues, for example

- on the proper evaluation of land's share in the overall housing stock for purposes of site value taxation,
- on misperceptions concerning the economic effects of current depreciation allowances,
- on whether the income tax treatment of maintenance investment is satisfying from an efficiency point of view.

Also included in chapter III is a comparison of the most important features of sales tax regulations in effect in the U.S., Canada, and West Germany.

II. The Laissez-Faire Economy and the Condition for an Efficient Allocation of Housing Capital and Building Land

The goal of this section is to derive conditions which can help to describe the efficient allocation. The second theorem of welfare economics states that these conditions are identical with the rules according to which in a tax-free economy landlords would plan their housing investment and landowners would plan the sale of building land, either one trying to maximize the market value of their enterprises.

The analysis starts at the point of time t_0. According to the decision of a superior planning authority made in t_0 there is an area of

(II.1) $B(t_0) > 0$

homogeneous units of vacant land which can be used for housing investment only, i.e. this land yields no non-housing benefits.

Moreover, in t_0 as the result of previous investment decisions there is a finite stock of homogeneous housing units

(II.2) $H(t_0) > 0.$

1. THE DECISION PROBLEM OF THE LANDLORD

In the planning period the representative landlord disposes of a stock of $H(t_0)$ homogeneous housing units which can be increased by further investment. Moreover, because of financing decisions made before t_0 the landlord has liabilities against the banking sector to the amount of

(II.3) $D(t_0) \lesseqgtr 0$.

New housing units can be produced by entrusting the exogenous construction firm with the erection of a house ready for (immediate) occupancy in a building lot of F^d square meters. The building lot was purchased before from the landowners at a price of P_B per square meter. The exogenous construction firm charges the price P_I for each of the service units provided. There exists a functional relationship between the newly-produced housing units and the inputs buildings land (F^d), and construction services (I)

(II.4) $h = f(I,F^d)$.

It is assumed that f is
- strictly quasi-concave,
- homogeneous of degree one,
- characterized by a constant elasticity of substitution $\sigma = -1$.

Given this, (II.4) can be rewritten as

$$h = F^d f(\frac{I}{F^d}, 1) = F^d \varphi(\varepsilon). \qquad \text{(II.5)}$$

In what follows, the variable ε is referred to as the <u>marginal capital intensity of land</u>. Consequently, the term $\varphi(\varepsilon)$ can be interpreted as the marginal <u>structural density of housing investment</u>. In addition it is assumed that the production in (II.5) is of the putty-clay type - housing investment is irreversible. Therefore, to change the capital intensity of a given building lot it is necessary to pull down the old building before a new, larger building can be erected. For the sake of simplicity the demolition cost are assumed to be prohibitively high. In these circumstances the landlord has to consider very carefully how much land he should develop today and which capital intensity he should choose; or even more whether it would not be better to postpone the development, meeting a higher future demand for housing services by erecting a larger building on the same lot at a later point of time. The economic intuition of this planning problem is provided by the following example.

Consider a landlord who wishes to acquire vacant land on which to provide newly constructed rental accomodation. Suppose also that there will be a once and for all increase in the demand for housing services in some future period. Knowing this, the landlord has several alternatives concerning the choice of time and density at which to build. The borderline cases are the following three:

1. to buy the building lot today and build a small structure on it in accordance with the present demand situation, foregoing higher future rental receipts;
2. to buy the building lot today and build on it a larger structure with a view to the future demand situation, accepting the possibility of vacant housing units today;
3. to postpone the purchase of the building lot and its development until the future increase in demand has occured, thus foregoing the rental receipts he would have otherwise received as well as avoiding the opportunity cost of housing investment during this time period.

A priori it is not clear which one of these alternatives the landlord will prefer; in the individual case this decision will depend upon the level of the interest rate, on how soon the demand change will occur, on the size of the change in the demand for housing services and on the level of the per-unit rent. But one statement can be made with certainty:
The greater is the future jump in housing demand, the more likely it is that alternative three will be chosen, i.e. that housing investment will be postponed.

The assumption about the irreversibility of housing investment is partially removed by the fact that the housing capital deteriorates as time goes on. Given that housing capital deteriorates at a constant rate δ over time*), the remaining units $h_t(t_0)$ of a single housing investment realized in a period $t < t_0$ are described by the following equation:

$$\text{(II.6)} \qquad h_t(t_0) = \exp[-\delta\alpha(t_0-t)]F^d(t)\varphi[\varepsilon(t)], \; 0 < \alpha < 1, \delta > 0.$$

In (II.6) α represents the production elasticity of construction services. Using (II.6) and neglecting maintenance investment as well as modernization investment, the total stock of housing units available in t_0 is

$$\text{(II.7)} \qquad H(t_0) = \int_{-\infty}^{t_0} \exp[-\delta\alpha(t_0-t)]F^d(t)\varphi[\varepsilon(t)]\,dt.$$

The partial differentiation of (II.7) with respect to time yields for $t = t_0$ the motion equation

$$\text{(II.8)} \qquad \dot{H}(t_o) = F^d(t_o)\varphi[\varepsilon(t_o)] - \alpha\delta H(t_o).\text{***)}$$

Obviously the change in the stock of housing units at a given point of time equals the difference between the newly produced housing units and the depreciation of this stock, caused by the deterioration of housing capital. Because (building) land does not deteriorate over time, the depreciation rate related to the stock of housing units is not equal to δ but to the product of δ and α , the production elasticity of construction services.

---

*) See Jorgenson (1967).

**) Equation (II.6) can be derived by considering that the assumptions concerning the construction technology imply a production function of the Cobb-Douglas type.

***) In what follows, $\dot{X}$ stands for the first derivative of the variable X with respect to time and $\hat{X} = \dot{X}/X$ for the relative change of X over time.

Equation (II.8) does not consider that the landlord principally always has the opportunity to compensate the loss in housing capital due to deterioration by adequate maintenance investment, or even overcompensate it by appropriate improvements. The distinction between maintenance investment and improvement is important. Maintenance investment in principle is reinvestment, for which the same cost-function holds as for the initial investment - provided that prices remain constant. If, for example, an old furnace is replaced by a new, but technically identical one, the cost for the purchase and the installation of the new equipment should be the same as for the old equipment. However, if the old heating is replaced by a new and technically more advanced one, additional costs will arise because of necessary constructional modifications at the building. Therefore the cost structure of improvements is completely different from that of maintenance investment.

Since the consideration of improvement investment would complicate our analysis greatly without providing any new result, the existence of this type of investment will be neglected in the following. The impact of this simplification on the decision problem of the landlord is that the stock of housing units can be widened only via new housing investment. With maintenance investment it is only possible to put already existing housing units in the state of newly produced housing units. E(t) denotes the quantity of maintenance investment at time t. Because of the irreversibility of housing investment and the statements made above, E (t) at each point of time has to fulfill the restrictions

$$\text{(II.9a)} \quad E(t) \geq 0, \qquad \text{if } H(t) < \overset{max}{H(t)} \;,$$

$$\text{(II.9b)} \quad 0 \leq E(t) \leq \alpha\delta\, H(t) \quad \text{if } H(t) = \overset{max}{H(t)}^{*)} .$$

The parameter $\overset{max}{H(t)}$ stands for the stock of housing units which would have occurred in period t if either there had been no depreciation or the worn out housing capital had been replaced completely in every period. H(t) represents the actual stock of housing units as the result of the actual investment and maintenance plan.

---

*) See Kamien/Schwartz (1981), pp. 215.

For this reason, motion equation (II.8) must be supplemented. The modified motion equation for the stock of housing units, considering the existence of maintenance investment, reads

$$(II.10) \quad \dot{H}(t_0) = F^d(t_0)\varphi[\varepsilon(t_0)] - [\alpha\delta H(t_0) - E(t_0)].$$

In accordance with the existing literature on housing economics, it is assumed that every housing unit existing at a given point of time delivers exactly one unit of housing services at the same point of time. Therefore H(t) also represents the flow of housing services produced at time t. These housing services are sold at a price of m dollars per unit per period to the sector of households, where m represents the households' marginal willingness to pay rent. This willingness depends on the supply H of housing services as well as on the level of demand for housing services; the parameter a serves as an index for this level. We assume the functional relationship

$$(II.11) \quad m(t) = m\left(\frac{a(t)}{H(t)}\right)$$

with the partial derivatives $m_H < 0$, $m_a > 0$ and a constant absolute price elasticity

$$(II.12) \quad \eta = \left|\frac{m \cdot H}{m' \cdot a}\right| = \text{constant} > 0.$$

It is unlikely that the parameter a remains constant over time. Because of the population growth and the accumulation of personal wealth from one generation to the other it is plausible to expect the per-household consumption of housing services to rise. With regard to this the parameter a is allowed to grow at a constant rate

$$(II.13) \quad \hat{a} = \text{constant} > 0$$

over time. This relationship is illustrated graphically by figure 2.

Figure 2

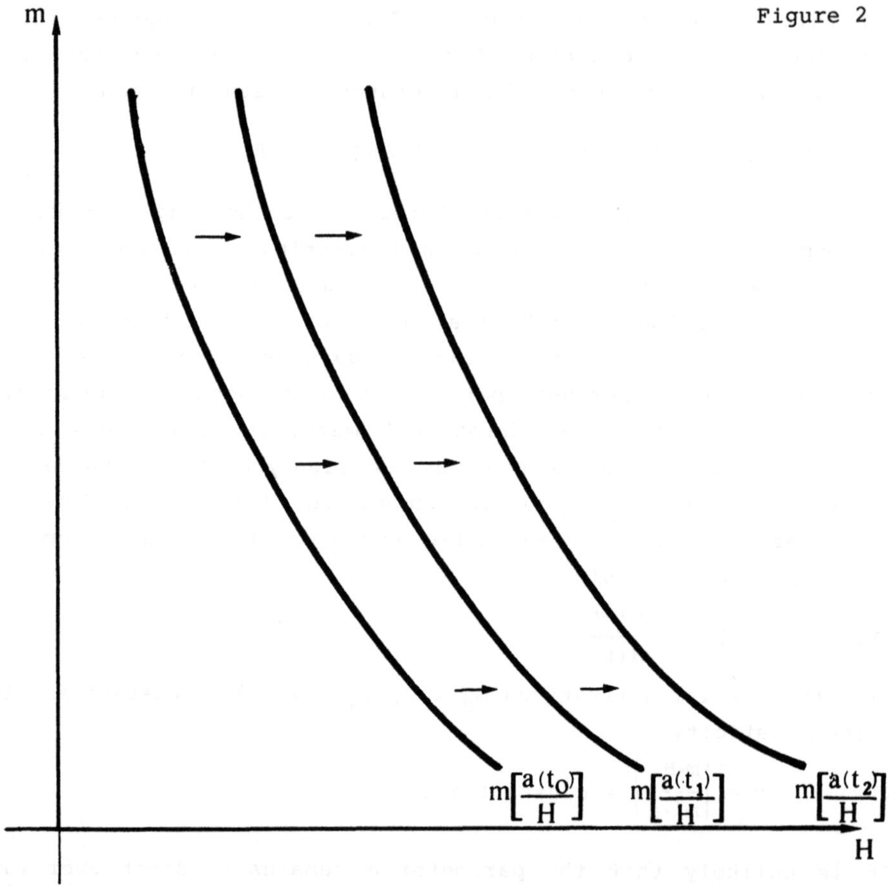

The demand for housing services is a decreasing function of the rental rate m. Under the influence of a continually increasing demand for housing services, the demand curve gradually shifts to the right.

In every period t the landlord achieves gross rental revenues of the value of m(t)H(t) dollars. To obtain the disposable cash flow of the landlord, we have to subtract the expenses for building land, for construction services, for interest liabilities, and for the net reduction of loans. This last flow is represented by the parameter S. Positive values of S are equivalent to an increase in the landlord's liabilities, D, as well as to an increase in the cash flow; negative values of S accordingly signal a decrease in both, his liabilities and his cash flow.

There is a limit to the landlord's credit. The banks certainly are not willing to grant loans which exceed the market value of equity tied in the stock H. To guarantee that this limit will not be surpassed, it is sufficient to assume that in each period the net increase in debt must not exceed the market value of net investment plus the capital gains accrued in the housing stock H in this period. Obviously the market value of net investment has to equal the present value of rental revenues earned by this investment. Let P_H denote the present value of rental revenues achievable by a single housing unit. Hence the landlord's financing plan has to fulfill the restriction

$$\text{(II.14)} \quad S \leq P_H \dot{H} + \dot{P}_H H = P_H \, [F^d \varphi(\varepsilon) - (\alpha\delta H - E)] + \dot{P}_H H.$$

There is no lower limit for the variable S: Nobody forbids the landlord to repay his debt or to buy bonds.

Proceeding on the conventions above the amount of money the landlord can distribute to the representative household in a given period is

$$\text{(II.15)} \quad A = mH - E - F^d \varepsilon - P_B F^d - rD + S.$$

In (II.15) the price of construction services, P_I, is chosen as "current" numéraire: at each point of time t (with $t_o \leq t \leq \infty$) P_I equals one.

According to Fisher's separation theorem it is assumed that the landlord tries to maximize the market value of equity tied in the stock of housing units. The market value is the most a potential purchaser would be willing to pay for this stock. This maximum value apparently depends on the advantages, i.e. the distributions, related to the possession of the housing stock. Hence, the market value of the housing stock is equivalent to the sum of present values of all the actual and future distributions it allows.

The maximum of the market value of equity contained in the stock H requires that the time paths for the net increase in debt, $\{S\}_{t_o}^{\infty}$, for maintenance investment, $\{E\}_{t_o}^{\infty}$, for the capital intensity of building land, $\{\varepsilon\}_{t_o}^{\infty}$, and for land consumption, $\{F^d\}_{t_o}^{\infty}$ are optimal. This optimization problem can be solved by using optimal control:

S, E, F^d and ε are the control variables, the stock of housing units, H, and the stock of liabilities, D, are the state variables. The motion equations corresponding to H and D are

(II.15) $\dot{H} = F^d \varphi(\varepsilon) - \alpha\delta H + E$

and

(II.16) $\dot{D} = S.$

Before the derivation of the necessary conditions for the landlord's planning problem can be dealt with, a problem of purely formal character has to be solved. One condition for the existence of a solution to the control problem mentioned above requires the continuity of state and costate variables - jumps in the stock of housing units as well as in the stock of vacant land are ruled out. Thus the existence of vacant land after t_o would be trivial. Since it is one goal of this analysis to examine whether the holding of - the "speculation" with - vacant land may be compatible with the welfare optimum, it is necessary to allow the possibility that all vacant land can be built upon at the planning date t_o.

To solve this problem we apply a formal trick.*) In addition to the real time an artificial time or "meta time" is introduced. As long as this meta-time runs, real time stands still. In this way it is possible to "stretch" a given point of (real) time and thus transform a discontinuous change in a state variable occurring in real time into a continuous process. Figure 3 illustrates this graphically for a jump in the stock of housing units taking place in t_o.

---

*) See Kamien/Schwartz (1981), pp. 226

Figure 3

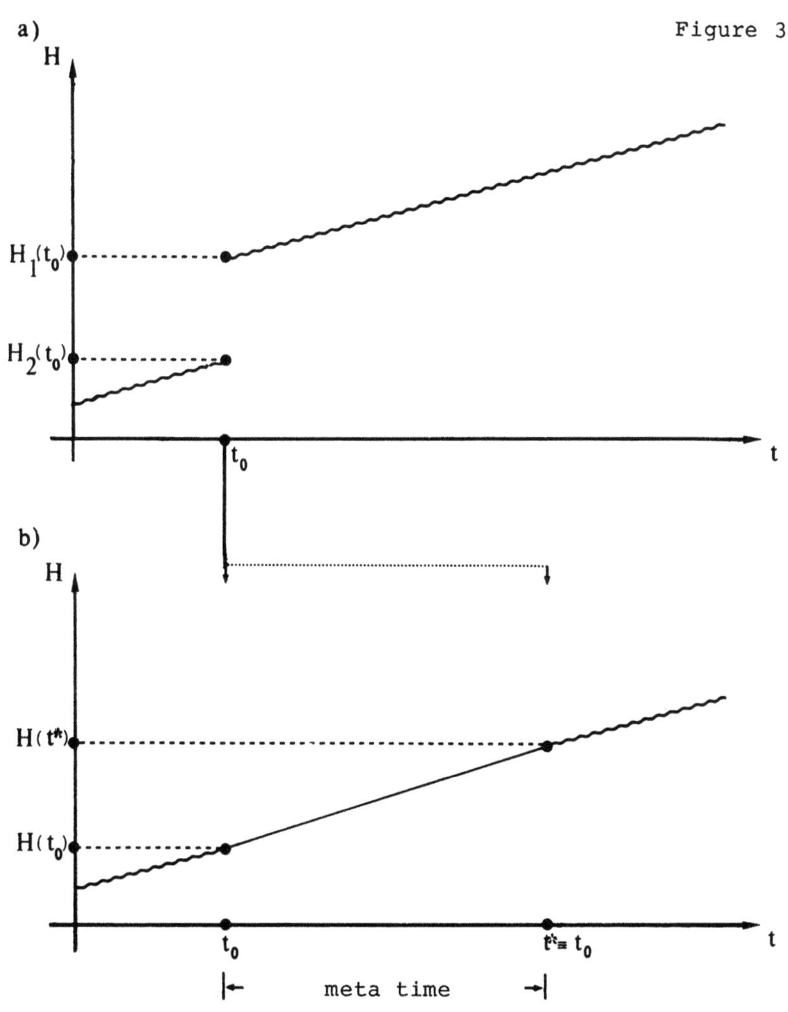

As long as the adjustment in the housing stock takes place, rental revenues are not realized, and depreciation-induced capital losses, expenses for maintenance, or interest payments do not occur. The only expenditures incurred in the meta-time period (t_o, t^*) are those for building land and construction services. Also the possibility of increases in liabilities has to be taken into account during (t_o, t^*). In what follows, the parameter z is used to indicate these facts. It is

$$\text{(II.17a)} \quad z = \begin{cases} 0 & \text{for } t_o \leq t < t^* \\ 1 & \text{for } t \geq t^* \end{cases} .$$

A similar problem arises in the context of maintenance investment. A continuous development of the housing stock would, given the time path of new housing investment, predetermine the time path of maintenance investment. A realistical discription of the dynamics of the market for old structures therefore requires the consideration of jumps in H triggered by discontinuities in maintenance plans. Suppose, that in a given point of time t_1 the landlord decides to renovate a certain fraction of the quantity of $H(t_1^{max}) - H(t_1)$ housing units. To transform the resulting jump in H into a steady process, the real time will be stopped in t_1 and the meta time will be started. When the adjustment process is finished in t^{**}, meta time stops and real time continues. During the meta time period (t_1, t^{**}) monetary streams can only be induced either by maintenance expenditures or by increases in the landlord's indebtedness. This is indicated by the parameter y, with

$$\text{(II.17b)} \quad y = \begin{cases} 0 & \text{for } t_1 \leq t < t^{**} \\ 1 & \text{for } t \geq t^{**} \end{cases} .$$

Giving heed to the conventions (II.17a) and (II.17b), the distributed profits in a given period are

$$\text{(II.18)} \quad A = yz(mH - rD) - y(F^d \varepsilon + P_B F^d) - zE + S.$$

Using (II.18), the landlord's decision problem can be described as follows:

$$\text{(II.19)} \quad \underset{\{S,E,F^d,\varepsilon\}}{\text{Max}} \quad M_H \equiv \int_{t_o}^{t_1} A(t)\exp[-yzr(t-\min(t_o,t^*)]\,dt$$

$$+\int_{t_1}^{\infty} A(t)\exp[-yzr(t-\min(t_1,t^{**})]\cdot\exp[-yzr(t_1-t^*)]\,dt,$$

under the constraints

$$\text{(II.2)} \quad H(t_o) > 0,$$

$$\text{(II.3)} \quad D(t_o) \gtrless 0,$$

$$\text{(II.9)} \quad E \begin{cases} \geq 0 \text{ for } H \leq H^{max} \\ \leq \alpha\delta H \text{ for } H = H^{max} \end{cases},$$

$$\text{(II.10)} \quad \dot{H} = yF^d \varphi(\varepsilon) - z(y\alpha\delta H - E).$$

$$\text{(II.14)} \quad S \leq P_H[yF^d \varphi(\varepsilon) - z(y\alpha\delta H - E)] + \dot{P}_H H,$$

$$\text{(II.16)} \quad \dot{D} = S,$$

$$\text{(II.17a)} \quad z = \begin{cases} 0 & \text{for } t_o \leq t < t^* \\ 1 & \text{for } t \geq t^* \end{cases},$$

$$\text{(II.17b)} \quad y = \begin{cases} 0 & \text{for } t_1 \leq t < t^{**} \\ 1 & \text{for } t \geq t^{**} \end{cases},$$

$$\text{(II.18)} \quad A = yz(mH - rD) - y(F^d \varepsilon + P_B F^d) - zE + S.$$

Equation (II.19) states the equivalence between the market value of equity tied in the housing stock and the present value of distributed earnings generated by the stock. Since the cash flows must not be discounted during meta time the parameters y and z appear in the exponent as well. The discount rate is the market interest rate r, which the landlord takes as given in his decision problem. For the sake of simplicity the interest rate is assumed to remain constant over time.

The Hamiltonian corresponding to the control problem in (II.19) reads

$$\text{(II.20)} \quad = yz(mH - rD) - y(F^d \varepsilon + P_B F^d) - zE + S$$
$$+ P_H[yF^d \varphi(\varepsilon) - z(y\alpha\delta H - E)]$$
$$+ \lambda_D S.$$

The variable P_H serves as shadow price of the housing stock; in the following P_H is referred to as house price. The parameter λ_D is the shadow value of the stock of liabilities.

The optimal values of the controls S, E, ε and F^d are those which maximize the value of the Hamiltonian at each point of time.

1.1 The Optimal Financing Decision

The first step to a solution of the landlord's decision problem is the choice of the optimal financing alternative.*

The landlord may finance his investment either with equity or with credit (equity financing will further on be denoted by the abreviation EF, credit financing by CF) or with an arbitrary combination of both. Equity financing includes financing with retained profits as well as financing by increasing the quantity of shares. In this last case, the parameter A in equation (II.18) has a negative sign.

To derive the optimal amount of debt financing, the Hamiltonian in equation (II.20) must be differentiated with respect to S. Because of the linearity of the Hamiltonian in S the possible solutions are

$$\text{(II.21)} \quad \frac{\partial \mathcal{H}}{\partial S} = 1 + \lambda_D \left\{ \begin{matrix} < \\ = \\ > \end{matrix} \right\} 0 \Rightarrow EF \left\{ \begin{matrix} > \\ \sim \\ < \end{matrix} \right\} CF.$$

Using the definition of the shadow value λ_D, we achieve

$$\text{(II.22)} \quad \lambda_D \equiv \frac{\partial M_H}{\partial D} = \int_{t_o}^{t_1} -yzr\cdot\exp[-yzr(t-t^*)]dt + \int_{t_1}^{\infty} -yzr\cdot\exp[-yzr(t-t^{**})]\exp[-yzr(t-t^*)]dt = -1$$

The substitution of (II.22) into (II.21) yields

$$\text{(II.23)} \quad \frac{\partial \mathcal{H}}{\partial S} = 0 \Rightarrow EF \sim CF.$$

---

*Unfortunately, the recent tax literature often neglects this close relationship between financing and investment decisions. In most cases a certain type of financing is assumed without considering whether this is the optimal, i.e. cheapest, alternative. This shortcoming frequently is the reason for misjudgements concerning the incidence of capital income taxation. (see, for example, the discussion of the corporation income tax incidence in Harberger (1963) and Sinn (1985b)).

Condition (II.23) states that <u>in a laissez-faire world with perfect capital markets the optimal financing plan is undeterminate</u> (provided that S varies within the boundaries defined in (II.14)).

The economic intuition behind this result is straightforward. To recognize this, one only has to think about the impacts a marginal change in the financing structure of the housing stock has on the firm owners' wealth. If one dollar of equity capital is replaced by a borrowed dollar, there will be an immediate one dollar increase in the distributions the households receive. Given the market interest rate, this additional dollar earns r dollars in interest income in every following period. On the other hand there will be a reduction in the households' income out of housing investment by the same amount, induced by an increase in interest liabilities of r dollar. Hence, the households' pecuniary circumstances remain unchanged. Realizing these relationships, the landlord is indifferent between the available financing alternatives.*)

1.2 <u>The Optimal Maintenance Plan</u>

The time path of maintenance investment determines the dynamics of the stock of old structures. Because of the linearity of equation (II.20) in E, the possibility of corner solutions has to be taken into account. The derivation of the optimal quantity of maintenance investment in a given period has to be based on the general optimality condition

$$\text{(II.24)} \quad \frac{\partial \mathcal{K}}{\partial E} = \frac{\partial \mathcal{K}}{\partial E} + \frac{\partial \mathcal{K}}{\partial S} \cdot \frac{\partial S}{\partial E} .$$

This is because according to (II.14) the landlord's credibility varies directly with E:

$$\text{(II.25)} \quad \frac{\partial S}{\partial E} = zP_H E.$$

---

*) In the literature the assumption is frequently made that the charged interest rate increases with the degree of indebtedness. As is shown by Hellwig (1981), an increase in the interest rate is not necessarily equivalent to an increase in the effective rate of interest, i.e. to a decline in the attractiveness of debt financing. See also Modigliani/Miller (1958), Sinn (1985b), section II.

But since the landlord cannot gain any benefit from this increase -it is $\partial\mathcal{H}/\partial S = 0$ - condition (II.24) reduces to

$$\text{(II.24)'} \quad \frac{\partial\mathcal{H}}{\partial E} = -yz + P_H \begin{Bmatrix} < \\ = \\ > \end{Bmatrix} 0 \Rightarrow E \begin{cases} = 0 \\ \geq 0 \\ = \alpha\delta H \end{cases} .$$

According to condition (II.24)', the landlord compensates the depreciation-induced losses in the housing stock only when there is a guarantee that the cost of maintenance is covered by the additional rental revenues made possible by maintenance. Condition (II.24)' requires this equivalence for the marginal unit of E: for $t>t^*$ it is $yz=1$, these are the per-unit cost of maintenance services. In turn, this marginal unit generates additional rental revenues worth P_H dollars, measured in present values. The definition of the houseprice P_H (the shadow value of the housing stock) implies

$$\text{(II.26)} \quad P_H(t_o) \equiv \frac{\partial M_H(t_o)}{\partial H(t_o)} = \frac{m\left[\frac{a(t_o)}{H(t_o)}\right]}{r + \alpha\delta}.$$

If the house price is less than one, it is not profitable for the landlord to maintain his housing stock. Maintenance investment becomes worthwhile at the moment t_1 where the houseprice equals or exceeds the value one. Exactly at this moment, a jump in the housing stock H can be observed, because the landlord now has an incentive to make up for all the maintenance he failed to carry out in the past. This discontinuous adjustment from $H(t_1)$ to $H(t_1)^{max}$ takes place in the meta time period (t_1, t^{**}). If P_H exceeds the value one beyond t^{**}, maintenance investment in every period $t > t_1$ is restricted to $E = \alpha\delta H$. As will be shown later the houseprice increases exponentially over time. Because it therefore inevitably will exceed the value one in a near future it is reasonable to assume $P_H > 1$ (and hence y=1) for all t, $t_o \leq t \leq \infty$. Consequently, the optimal maintenace plan in a tax-free world reads

$$\text{(II.27)} \quad E = \begin{cases} 0 & \text{for } t_o \leq t < t^* \\ \alpha\delta H & \text{for } t \geq t^* \end{cases} .$$

Within the whole planning horizon (t_o,∞) all depreciation-induced losses in the housing stock H will be compensated by appropriate maintenance measures.

1.3 The Optimal New Housing Investment Plan

The optimal decision concerning the construction of new housin units includes the optimal choice of the time path of lan consumption, $\{F^d\}_{t_o}^{\infty}$ as well as of the time path of the capita intensity of land, $\{\varepsilon\}_{t_o}^{\infty}$. Taking into account the influence c financing decisions on investment plans, we have to proceed fr the necessary conditions

$$\text{(II.28)} \quad \frac{\partial \mathcal{K}}{\partial \varepsilon} = \frac{\partial \mathcal{K}}{\partial \varepsilon} + \frac{\partial \mathcal{H}}{\partial S}\frac{\partial S}{\partial \varepsilon},$$

$$\text{(II.29)} \quad \frac{\partial \mathcal{H}}{\partial F^d} = \frac{\partial \mathcal{H}}{\partial F^d} + \frac{\partial \mathcal{H}}{\partial S}\frac{\partial S}{\partial F^d},$$

$$\text{(II.30)} \quad -\frac{\partial \mathcal{H}}{\partial H} = -\left[\frac{\partial \mathcal{H}}{\partial H} + \frac{\partial \mathcal{K}}{\partial S}\frac{\partial S}{\partial H}\right].$$

Because of the financing boundary formulated in (II.14), th following partial derivatives hold:

$$\text{(II.31)} \quad \frac{\partial S}{\partial \varepsilon} = P_H F^d \varphi'(\varepsilon),$$

$$\text{(II.32)} \quad \frac{\partial S}{\partial F^d} = P_H \varphi(\varepsilon),$$

$$\text{(II.33)} \quad \frac{\partial S}{\partial H} = -P_H \alpha\delta + \dot{P}_H.$$

Investment in new structures and capital gains accrued in the housing stock raise and capital losses (due to depreciation) deminish the landlord's credibility. In a tax-free world, the conditions (II.28)-(II.30) can be reduced because of the landlord's financing indifference, implying $\partial\mathcal{H}/\partial S = 0$. Therefore, since the production function is assumed to be strictly quasi-concave, the necessary condition for the optimal capital intensity is

(II.34) $\frac{\partial \mathcal{H}}{\partial \varepsilon} \overset{!}{=} 0 = -F^d + F^d P_H \varphi'(\varepsilon),$

from which

(II.35) $P_H \varphi'(\varepsilon) = 1$

follows straightforwardly. Condition (II.35) requires that in the optimum <u>the margianal value product of construction services has to equal the price of the marginal service unit.</u>

Since the Hamiltonian in (II.20) is linear with respect to F^d, we obtain the following optimality condition for land consumption:

(II.36) $P_H \varphi(\varepsilon) - \varepsilon \left\{\begin{matrix} < \\ = \end{matrix}\right\} P_B \Rightarrow F^d \left\{\begin{matrix} = \\ \geq \end{matrix}\right\} 0$

Condition (II.36) states that <u>it depends on the difference between the marginal value product of land</u>*) <u>and the per-unit price of land, P_B, in a given period whether there will be land transactions (and therefore construction activities) in this period</u>. Since the marginal value product of land is equivalent to the landlord's marginal willingness to pay for land, sales of building land will occur in real time only when both terms are equal.

In (II.36), the case $\partial \mathcal{H}/\partial F^d > 0$ is ruled out. The reason is that this case is not compatible with the optimal solution for the Hamiltonian. As long as the marginal value product of land exceeds the price of land, there will be an unlimited incentive for the landlord to buy vacant land and build on it.

Condition (II.36) can be simplified; using the fact that the production function in (II.5) boasts constant partial production elasticities, the partial production elasticity of capital is:

(II.38) $\alpha = \frac{\varphi'(\varepsilon)}{\varphi(\varepsilon)} \varepsilon = \text{constant} > 0.$

---

*) Considering condition (II.35) it is

$\partial[P_H F^d \varphi(\varepsilon)]/\partial F^d = P_H \varphi(\varepsilon) - P_H F^d \varphi'(\varepsilon)[\frac{I}{(F^d)^2}]$

$= P_H \varphi(\varepsilon) - P_H \varphi'(\varepsilon)\varepsilon$

$= P_H \varphi(\varepsilon) - \varepsilon .$

Using the parameter β to denote the production elasticity of land and referring to the assumption that the production function is homogeneous of degree one, (II.36) can be rewritten in regard to (II.35) as

$$(II.38) \quad \frac{\beta}{\alpha} \; \varepsilon \begin{Bmatrix} < \\ = \\ \end{Bmatrix} P_B \;\Rightarrow\; F^d \begin{Bmatrix} = \\ \geq \end{Bmatrix} 0$$

Condition (II.38) contains a crucial implication for further analysis: the choice of the capital intensity of land depends on the relation between the price of land and the price of construction services (P_I is used as numéraire) as well as on the ratio of the production elasticities. But, since α and β are assumed to be constant, the dynamic development of ε only depends on the dynamic behaviour of the price ratio P_B.

The third necessary condition for the construction optimum is

$$(II.39) \quad -\frac{\partial \mathcal{H}}{\partial H} = \dot{P}_H - zrP_H = -z(m - \alpha\delta P_H).$$

Rearranging terms and referring to the definition of the meta-time variable z yields the equilibrium growth rate of the house price:

$$(II.40a) \quad \hat{P}_H = 0 \qquad \text{for } t_o \leq t < t^*,$$

$$(II.40b) \quad \hat{P}_H = -\frac{m}{P_H} + r + \alpha\delta \qquad \text{for } t \geq t^*.$$

Equation (40b) is the familiar condition for an intertemporal arbitrage equilibrium: the value of assets tied in the housing sector is the optimal when the last dollar invested in a structure earns the same (net) return the alternative investment in bonds would have earned. The (net) return on the marginal housing investment is equal to the pecuniary rate of return, $\frac{m}{P_H}$, plus the capital gain, $\hat{P}_H$, and less the depreciation induced capital loss, $\alpha\delta$, of the housing unit financed with the marginal dollar. Solving (II.40b) for m/P_H yields the well known user-cost-of-capital formula.

Condition (40a) requires the house price to remain constant during the meta-time period (t_o, t^*). Otherwise the conditions (II.40a) and (II.40b) could not describe an equilibrium; for example, if $\hat{P}_H(t) > 0$, $t_o \leq t < t^*$, it would be worthwhile for the households to readjust their portfolio during (t_o, t^*) in favour of real estate, because wealth tied in bonds by definition does not earn interest during this period.
Finally, the optimal investment decision has to fulfill the transversality condition

$$\text{(II.43)} \quad \lim_{t\to\infty} [P_H(t)H(t)\exp(-r(t-t_o))] = 0.$$

2. THE DECISION PROBLEM OF THE LANDOWNER

In the previous section the landlord's decision problem is described under the assumption that the decision concerning the supply of buildung land has already been made. This section describes the economic factors that influence this decision.

Since vacant land by assumption yields no intermediate benefits, the sale of vacant land is the landowner's sole source of revenue. In accordance with the separation theorem, the landowner chooses the time path of land supply, $\{F^S\}_{t_o}^{\infty}$, that maximizes the present value of land sale revenues. Since the landowner by assumption is a perfect competitor, taking the market price P_B as given in his decision problem, the present value M_B of sale revenues is

$$\text{(II.44)} \quad M_B(t_o) \equiv \int_{t_o}^{\infty} P_B(t)F^S(t)\exp[-zr(t-t^*)]\,dt.$$

The solution to this problem can be obtained by applying optimal control. The stock of vacant land, B, is the state variable and the supply of vacant land, F^S, the control variable. Since housing investment is irreversible and demolition costs are prohibitively high, the stock B follows the motion equation

$$\text{(II.45)} \quad \dot{B} = -F^S, \; F^S \geq 0.$$

The algebraical description of the landowner's decision problem is

(II.46) $\underset{\{F^S\}}{\text{Max}} \; M_B(t_o)$

under the constraints

(II.1) $B(t_o) > 0,$

(II.17) $z = \begin{cases} 0 & \text{for } t_o \leq t < t^* \\ 1 & \text{for } t \geq t^* \end{cases},$

(II.45) $\dot{B} = -F^S.$

The corresponding Hamiltonian reads

(II.47) $\mathcal{H} = P_B F^S - \lambda_B F^S.$

In (II.47) the parameter λ_B represents the shadow price of the stock of vacant land. The necessary conditions for an optimum can be derived by partially differentiating the Hamiltonian with respect to F^S and B, considering the canonical equation for B. These operations yield in the case of an interior solution for F^S

(II.48) $\lambda_B = P_B,$

(II.49) $\dot{\lambda}_B - zr\lambda_B = 0.$

The substitution of equation (II.48) into equation (II.49) results in the following optimality conditions:

(II.50a) $\hat{P}_B = 0$ for $t_o \leq t < t^*,$

(II.50b) $\hat{P}_B = r$ for $t \geq t^*.$

Condition (II.50a) is the counterpart to equation (II.40a) in the landlord's decision problem, requiring the constancy of the land price during the meta-time period.

The more interesting condition is condition (II.50b). It requires that in an equilibrium situation <u>in which transactions of vacant</u>

land occur the land price has to grow at a rate equal to the market interest rate. Condition (II.50) features the well-known Hotelling-rule for the depletion of exhaustible resources.*)

The economic background of this rule is easy to describe. As is known from the decision problem in section II.1., it perhaps may be beneficial to the landlord to postpone the purchase and development of building land in order to match a higher future demand for housing services. Obviously the realization of this plan resumes the landowner's willingness to keep the required building land in his stock B until it is needed. But even obvious this willingness depends on whether the landlord himself is willing to compensate the landowner for all opportunity cost, i.e. forgone interest, incurred in the holding of vacant land. The landlord's marginal willingness to pay for land has to grow at least at the rate r in order to make land "speculation" profitable. If the landlord's willingness to pay grows at a lower rate than r--for example because the expectations about the future demand situation in the rental market are rather pessimistic--it is rational for the landowner to sell his whole stock of vacant land immediately and to invest the sale receipts in the capital market at the going interest rate r. However, if the percentage increase in the willingness to pay is higher than the interest rate--for example, because the expectations about the future demand for housing services are optimistic--the most profitable strategy now is to postpone any sale of vacant land to a future period where condition (II.50b) again holds. These reflections allow for the following proposition: In a laissez-faire world transactions of vacant land as well as construction activities can be observed only at such (real) points of time where the market price of vacant land grows at a rate equal to the market interest rate.

The third necessary condition for the existence of a solution to the landowner's decision problem is the transversality condition

$$\text{(II.51)} \quad \lim_{t \to \infty} \{P_B(t)B(t)\exp[-r(t-t_o)]\} = 0 .$$

*) See Hotelling (1931).

3. CONDITIONS FOR THE MARKET EQUILIBRIUM - FEATURES OF A PARETO-OPTIMAL ALLOCATION

The results described in the preceding sections allow for the formulation of conditions characterizing the equilibria in the rental market, the market for housing construction and the building land market. According to the second theorem of welfare economics, these conditions together are necessary conditions for the existence of a welfare optimum.

As mentioned earlier, the time paths of the rental rate, $\{m\}_{t_o}^{\infty}$, and the land price, $\{P_B\}_{t_o}^{\infty}$, are endogeneous variables that adjust such that the plans of all agents are compatible at every single point of time. In analytical terms this compatibility is guarenteed if the optimality conditions for the individual decision problems are fulfilled simultaneously and the markets in question are cleared at every single point of time.

In particular, this implies that the demand for housing services has to meet the supply of such services for all $t \in (t^*,\infty)$, i.e.

$$\text{(II.52)} \quad m = m(\frac{a}{H}),$$

that the market for vacant land is cleared for all $t \in (t^*,\infty)$, i.e.

$$\text{(II.53)} \quad F^d = F^s = F,$$

and that the succeeding conditions are fulfilled simultaneously:

$$\text{(II.54)} \quad z \begin{Bmatrix} > \\ = \\ < \end{Bmatrix} P_H \Rightarrow E \begin{cases} = 0 \\ \geq 0 \\ = \alpha\delta H \end{cases} \qquad \text{for } t \geq t_o$$

$$\text{(II.55)} \quad \varepsilon = \varepsilon^* \qquad \text{for } F > 0 \text{ and } t \geq t^*,$$

where ε^* is implicitly defined through

$$\text{(II.56)} \quad P_H \varphi'(\varepsilon^*) = 1 \qquad \text{for } t \geq t_o,$$

$$\text{(II.57)} \quad \frac{\beta}{\alpha} \varepsilon^* \begin{Bmatrix} < \\ = \end{Bmatrix} P_B \Rightarrow F \begin{Bmatrix} = \\ \geq \end{Bmatrix} 0 \qquad \text{for } t \geq t_o,$$

(II.58) $\hat{P}_H = -\frac{m}{P_H} + r + \alpha\delta$ for $t \geq t^*$,

(II.59) $\hat{P}_H = \hat{P}_B = 0$ for $t_o \leq t < t^*$,

(II.60) $\hat{P}_B = r$ for $t \geq t^*$,

(II.61) $\lim_{t\to\infty} \{P_X(t)X(t)\exp[-zr(t-t_o)]\} = 0$, $X = H, B$.

In regard of the dynamic objective of this analysis it is important to know that conditions (II.52) - (II.61) do not merely describe a family of static equilibria, but implicitly also the intertemporal equilibrium trajectory of the model economy. It is the dynamic behaviour of the demand for housing services that is responsible for the economy's advance on this path.

4. MODEL DYNAMICS

The growth in the demand for housing services has a direct impact on the rental rate, m, and the house price, P_H. Differentiating (II.26) with respect to time and dividing this partial differential by P_H, we obtain

(II.62) $\hat{P}_H = \frac{\hat{a}-\hat{H}}{\eta}$.

In (II.62) η denotes the numerical value of the price elasticity of demand for housing services. As is stated by (II.62) the percentage change of the rental rate or the houseprice, respectively, is a direct function of the relative change between the demand for and the supply of housing services.

Equation (II.62) also implies that there is an upper boundary for the percentage change of the house price over time. Given the assumptions concerning the irreversibility of housing investment and the value of P_H ($P_H > 1$, implying $E = \alpha\delta H$), this boundary is reached when there are no construction activities ($\hat{H} = 0$), i.e. when the market clearing can be achieved by a rise in the rental rate only. Hence, the maximum growth rate of the house price is

$$\hat{P}_H^{max} = \frac{\hat{a}}{\eta} . \tag{II.63}$$

According to optimality condition (II.56) the rise in the demand for housing services also influences the choice of the capital intensity of land. Referring to the assumption that the production function in (II.5) is characterized by a constant elasticity of substitution $\sigma = -1$, and applying some straightforward calculations in (II.56), we obtain*)

$$\hat{P}_H = \beta\hat{\varepsilon}. \tag{II.64}$$

Equation (II.64) states that the capital-intensity of land grows in proportion to the house price, but (because of $0 < \beta < 1$) at a higher rate.

Similarly, increasing revenues have an impact on the landlord's marginal willingness to pay for building land. From condition (II.56) it follows that in equilibrium the marginal willingness to pay grows at the same rate as the price of land does, implying

$$\hat{\varepsilon} = \hat{P}_B . \tag{II.65}$$

As a consequence of the relationships stated in equations (II.63) and (II.64), there also has to be an upper boundary for $\hat{\varepsilon}$:

$$\hat{\varepsilon}^{max} = \frac{\hat{a}}{\eta\beta}. \tag{II.66}$$

However, it is by no means sufficient to show the impact of the demand for housing services on the landlord's investment decision if one wants to describe the dynamics of the stock of housing units and the stock of vacant land. Decisive for the intertemporal development of these stocks as well is whether the landowner intends to support the landlord's investment plans by an appropriate planing of his land sales.

---

*) Because of $\sigma = -1$ the elasticity of φ' with respect to ε is identical to the production elasticity of land:
(i) $\beta = -[\varphi''(\varepsilon)/(\varphi'(\varepsilon)]\varepsilon$.

Consider a scenario where in the planning period t_o, the marginal value product of land equals the desired land price P_B. Suppose also that there will be only slight future increases in the demand for housing services, so that even in the case where there are no construction activities (i.e. $\hat{H} = 0$) the marginal willingness to pay for land grows at a rate which does not exceed the market interest rate. Because $\hat{\varepsilon} = \hat{\varepsilon}^{max} \leq \hat{P}_B = r$ holds and because of equations (II.65) and (II.66), the growth in demand then fulfills the restriction

$$\text{(II.67)} \quad \hat{a} \leq \eta\beta\hat{P}_B = \eta\beta r.$$

In this situation there is no incentive for the landowner to offer building land beyond t_o, since in no period after t_o the realizable land price would be sufficient to cover the opportunity cost incurred in the holding of land. Given (II.67) the optimal selling plan obviously requires that all vacant land available in the planning period has to be sold in that period. In terms of our analysis, the stock $B(t_o)$ of vacant land will be sold and built upon with the capital intensity $\varepsilon(t_o)$ during the meta-time period (t_o, t^*) - an event, that in real time can be interpreted as a <u>short-run construction boom</u>. After t_o there won't be any construction activities. The semi-logarithmic graph in figure 4 illustrates these relationships graphically.

Figure 4

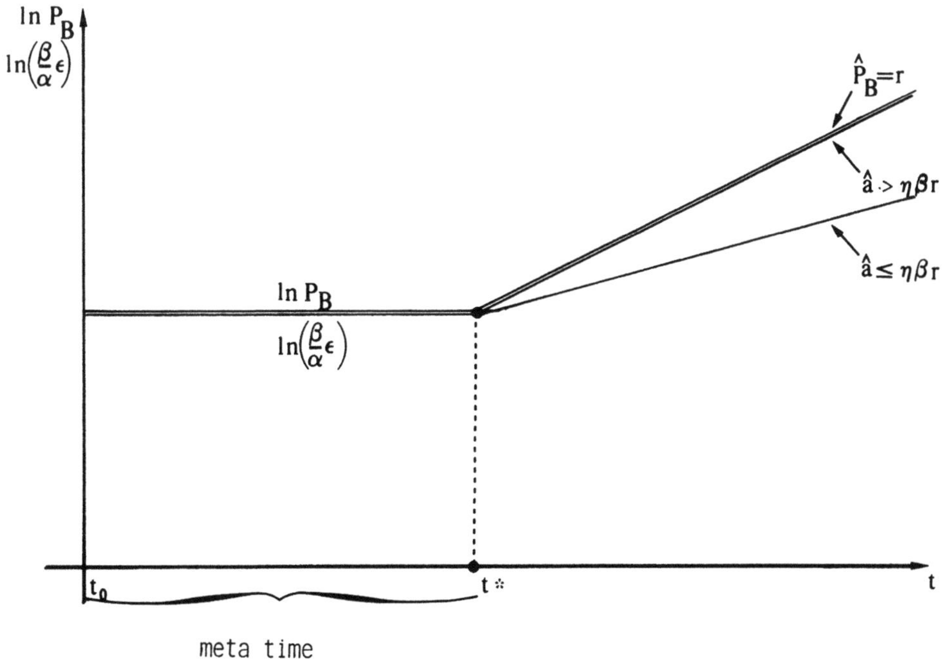

The curves $\ln(P_B)$ and $\ln(\frac{\beta}{\alpha}\varepsilon)$ describe the development of the land price and the marginal value product of land, respectively, with respect to time. According to condition (II.59) and the assumed scenario, both curves have a zero slope and coincide during the meta-time period. Hence, during (t_o, t^*) condition (II.57) holds with equality, implying land transactions as well as construction activities within this period. After the end of meta time both curves branch off for $\hat{a} < \eta\beta r$, implying that the marginal willingness to pay falls short of the cost covering land price for the rest of the planning period. And even in the case, where

$\hat{a} = \eta\beta r$ and hence $\hat{\varepsilon}^{max} = \hat{P}_B$ holds, there will be no land transactions and construction activities beyond t^*. To see this, suppose investment in new housing units occurs after t^*. Then, because of $\hat{H} > 0$, $\hat{\varepsilon} < \hat{\varepsilon}^{max} = \hat{P}_B$ would hold, implying $\frac{\beta}{\alpha}\varepsilon < P_B$ and F=0, an obvious contradiction to the initial assumption.

The statement that <u>all</u> vacant land will be built upon during the meta-time period is confirmed by the model's solution: if only a part of the stock $B(t_o)$ were built upon during (t_o, t^*) then, since there are no sales of vacant land after t^*, $\lim_{t\to\infty} B(t) > 0$ would hold. Because the Hotelling rule requires $\hat{P}_B = r$, the transversality condition (II.61) could be fulfilled only if $P_B(t_o) = 0$. On the other hand the house price $P_H(t_o)$ is bigger than zero because the quantity of housing units $H(t_o)$ is finite. As can be seen from conditions (II.56) and (II.57), a positive house price implies a strictly positive marginal value product of land. Therefore, $\lim_{t\to\infty} B(t) > 0$ is only compatible with a scenario in which the willingness to pay for land initially exceeds the price of land. As was shown earlier, such a constellation violates the existence condition for a solution to the landlord's decision problem.

Beyond t^* sales of vacant land and construction activities only occur if the growth rate of the demand for housing services satisfies the condition

$$\text{(II.68)} \quad \hat{a} > \eta\beta\hat{P}_B = \eta\beta r,$$

implying $\hat{\varepsilon}^{max} > \hat{P}_B$. In this case the time paths of the desired land price P_B and the marginal value product of land coincide over the whole planning horizon (t_o, ∞). This coincidence is required by the optimality conditions (II.52)-(II.61). The situation, where the path for the marginal value product of land runs above the path of the land price can be excluded; otherwise conditions (II.52)-(II.61) could not describe the maximum of the Hamiltonian in (II.20). Equally impossible is that the $\ln(\frac{\alpha}{\beta}\varepsilon)$ path is located below the $\ln P_B$ path; otherwise, since $\frac{\alpha}{\beta}\varepsilon < P_B$ all land transactions would be suspended; from $\hat{H} = 0$ it follows that $\hat{\varepsilon} = \hat{\varepsilon}^{max} > \hat{P}_B = r$: even the slightest downward deviation of the $\ln(\frac{\beta}{\alpha}\varepsilon)$ path would be corrected immediately by an acceleration in the growth of the marginal value product of land.

The coincidence of both paths implies that in each period after t^* vacant land will exist, i.e. that the stock of vacant land, B, will not be exhausted in finite time. This conclusion can be proven by using the optimality conditions in section II.3. Suppose it is optimal to develop the whole stock B until a period t^{**}, with $t^* < t^{**} < \infty$. Consequently the stock of housing units would remain constant after t^{**}. From $\hat{H} = 0$ follows that $\hat{\varepsilon} = \hat{\varepsilon}^{max} > \hat{P}_B = r$. Thus in each period beyond t^{**} the marginal value product of land would exceed the price P_B of land, again violating the conditions for the existence of an optimal solution.

The previous arguments refer to a situation in which initially the marginal willingness to pay for land equals the desired price of land. This assumption is arbitrary. The situation in which the marginal willingness to pay falls short of the demand price is just as likely to occur. In this situation as well, the answer to the question whether or not vacant land will exist beyond t^* depends on the development of the demand for housing services.

At first glance one is tempted to assume that in a situation in which the landlord is not willing to pay the demanded land price the sale of land is out of question. But this impression is wrong. If the demand for housing services increases relative slightly at a rate

$$\text{(II.67)} \quad \hat{a} \leq \eta \beta . r,$$

the landlord's most profitable strategy always is to sell the whole stock of vacant land in the planning period at the price

$$\text{(II.69)} \quad \tilde{P}_B(t_o) = \frac{\beta}{\alpha}\varepsilon(t_o) < P_B(t_o)$$

instead of postponing the sale: the longer the sale is postponed, the bigger the difference will be between the cost-covering price P_B and the realizable price $\tilde{P}_B$. This is shown in figure 5a.

Figure 5 a

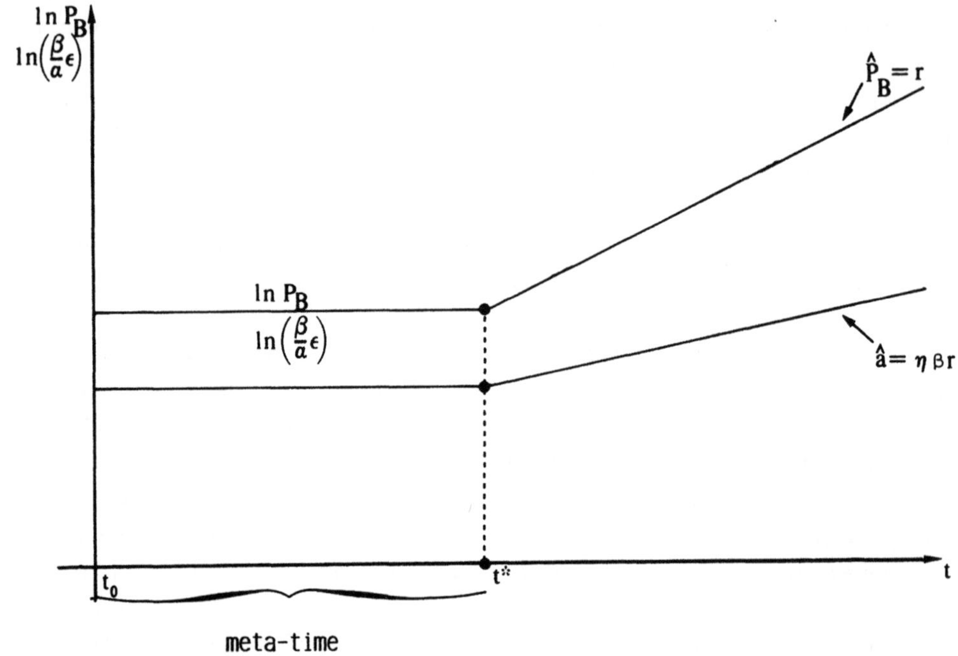

As in the case of figure 4 transactions of vacant land and hence construction activities occur in the meta-time period only. Again, housing investment beyond t^* is restricted to maintenance investment.

Obviously the condition $\hat{a} > \eta\beta r$ is once more a necessary condition for the existence of vacant land beyond t^*. The landowner refuses to sell his whole stock B in t_o only if he has reason to assume that in some future period $t^{**} > t^*$ the landlord is willing to pay the price $P_B(t^{**}) = P_B(t^*)\exp[r(t^{**}-t^*)]$ for each unit of vacant land. Figure 5b features the conditions for the occurrence of such a situation. According to condition (II.59) during the meta-time period the paths for the land price and the marginal willingness to pay for land can be described by horizontal lines, whereby the $\ln P_B$ - path by assumption lies above the $\ln(\frac{\alpha}{\beta}\varepsilon)$ - path. The condition for both paths to meet in finite time is that during a transition period (t^*, t^{**}) the $\ln(\frac{\alpha}{\beta}\varepsilon)$ - path boasts a steeper slope than the $\ln P_B$ - path. Since there are no construction activities during (t^*, t^{**}), the growth rate of the marginal value product then adopts its maximum value. From the requirement $\hat{\varepsilon} = \hat{\varepsilon}^{max} > \hat{P}_B = r$ it follows that the demand for housing services has to grow at a rate satisfying

(II.68) $\hat{a} > \eta\beta\hat{P}_B = \eta\beta r.$

In figure 5b both paths meet in t^{**}, after which they coincide for the rest of the planning period.

Figure 5 b

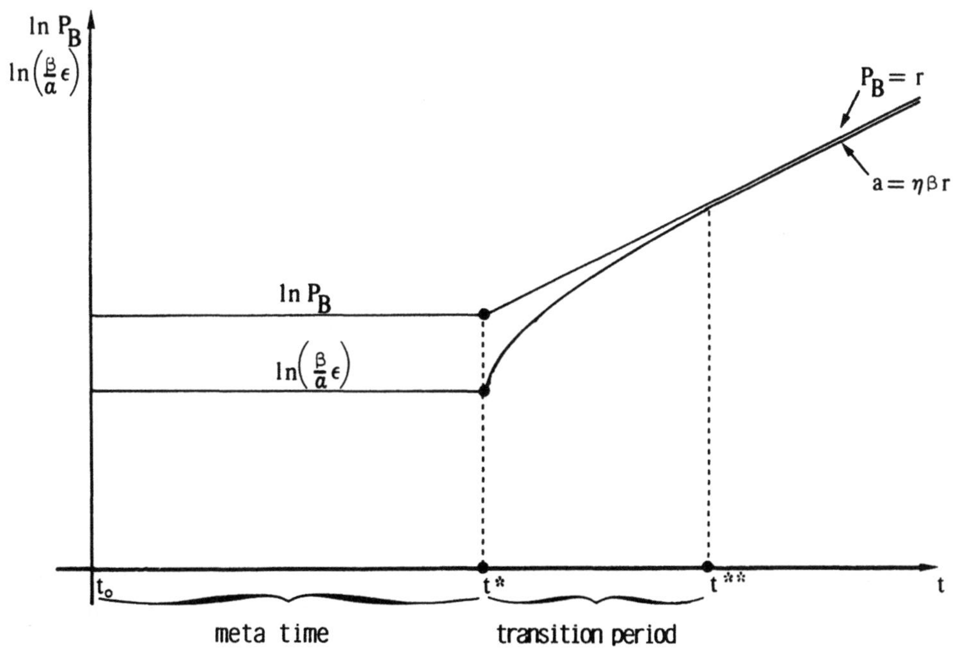

The assertion that a deviation between both paths will not occur after t^{**} can be proven by applying the same formal steps used in commenting on figure 4. In equilibrium land supply and land demand adjust such that the landlord in each period after t^{**} is willing to pay the desired price P_B. Hence, land transactions as well as construction activities will be observable in each period after t^{**}, implying once more that the stock of vacant land will not be exhausted in finite time. This last conclusion is confirmed by optimality conditions (II.56), (II.57) and (II.61).

We can summarize the prevailing discussion concerning the dynamics of the laissez-faire economy as follows:

Permanent increases in the stock of housing units require a sufficiently fast rising demand for housing services. The borderline growth rate that just fails to satisfy this requirement is determined by the product of the absolute price elasticity of rental demand, η, the land share in construction cost, β, and the opportunity cost of holding vacant land, r. After a possible transition period, the pareto-optimal trajectory of the laissez-faire economy is characterized by a continuous increase in the housing stock, H, the house price, P_H, the rental rate, m, the land price, P_B, and the capital intensity of land, ε. The stock of vacant land shrinks steadily over time, but will never be exhausted in finite time.

These preliminary results provide a first criterion for the evaluation of actual housing policies. At least in the case of a relatively fast increasing demand for housing services, a policy urging for a fast development of vacant land would be suboptimal. For the decision whether the owners of vacant land should be induced by government intervention to provide more building land than they previously did, expectations about the future rental demand ought to be as important as the present demand conditions.

For the further analysis the case of a relatively slow increasing demand for housing services is of minor interest. In what follows an economy is dealt with in which the growth of rental demand satisfies condition (II.68). This implies that at least after a possible transition period the conditions for the occurrence of permanent construction activities

(II.70) $\frac{\beta}{\alpha}\varepsilon = P_B$,

and

(II.71) $\hat{\varepsilon} = \hat{P}_B$

also hold.

Substituting (II.71) into (II.62) and considering (II.64) yields the equilibrium growth rate for the stock of housing units:

(II.72) $\hat{H} = \hat{a} - \eta\beta\hat{P}_B = \text{constant} > 0.$

Equation (II.72) confirms that there will be investment in new housing only if the demand for rental accomodation grows at some minimum rate $\hat{a} > \eta\beta\hat{P}_B$.

Equation (II.72) also allows for conclusions concerning the dynamics of the stock of vacant land. Because of the constancy stated in equation (II.72), the equality $\hat{H} = \hat{\dot{H}}$ follows straightforwardly. Furthermore, the price of a housing unit, P_H, by assumption exceeds the cost of one maintenance service unit, implying that the worn out housing capital will be replaced instantly and completely in each period beyond t^*. Therefore it follows from motion equation

(II.10) $\dot{H} = F\varphi(\varepsilon) - z(\alpha\delta H - E)$

that the housing stock, H, grows at a rate

(II.73) $\hat{H} = \hat{\dot{H}} = \hat{\varphi} + \hat{F} = \alpha\,\hat{\varepsilon} + \hat{F}.$

The substitution of (II.73) into (II.72) results in the growth rate for vacant land consumption:

(II.74) $\hat{F} = \hat{a} - \hat{P}_B(\eta\beta + \alpha) = \text{constant} < 0$*) .

---

*) That the consumption of vacant land decreases over time can be proven by using the transversality condition for the state variable H. Condition (II.61) requires

(i) $\hat{H} + \hat{P}_H - r < 0.$

Substituting (i) into (II.72) and considering the Hotelling-rule stated in (II.60), one obtains the negative sign for the parameter $\hat{F}$.

Considering $dF/dB = \dot{F}/\dot{B}$, it follows from the motion equation of the stock of vacant land that

$$\text{(II.75)} \quad \frac{dF}{dB} = \frac{\dot{F}}{F} = \hat{F} > 0.$$

According to (II.75) land consumption is a linear function of the stock of vacant land, describable by the general equation $F = b_1 + b_2 B$, with b_1, b_2 = constant, $b_2 > 0$. But it turns out that in the general equation $b_1 = 0$ has to hold: $b_1 > 0$ would imply that the stock of vacant land will be depleted in finite time, $b_1 < 0$ would require that a part of the stock of vacant land will never be developed. As was shown earlier both cases violate the existence condition for a solution to the planning problems discussed in the previous sections.

From $b_1 = 0$ it follows that $\hat{F} = \hat{B}$ or

$$\text{(II.76)} \quad \hat{B} = \hat{a} - \hat{P}_B(\eta\beta + \alpha) = \text{constant} < 0.$$

The equations (II.72) and (II.76) can be used for the derivation of common trajectories of the state variables H and B. In a (H,B)-plane both equations describe a family of rectangular hyperbolas with the slope

$$\text{(II.77)} \quad \frac{dH}{dB} = \frac{\dot{H}}{\dot{B}} = \frac{H[\hat{a} - \eta\beta\hat{P}_B]}{B[\hat{a} - (\eta\beta + \alpha)\hat{P}_B]} < 0.$$

In the right quadrant of figure 6 the hyperbolas AA, CC, DD and EE are four representatives of this family.

Figure 6

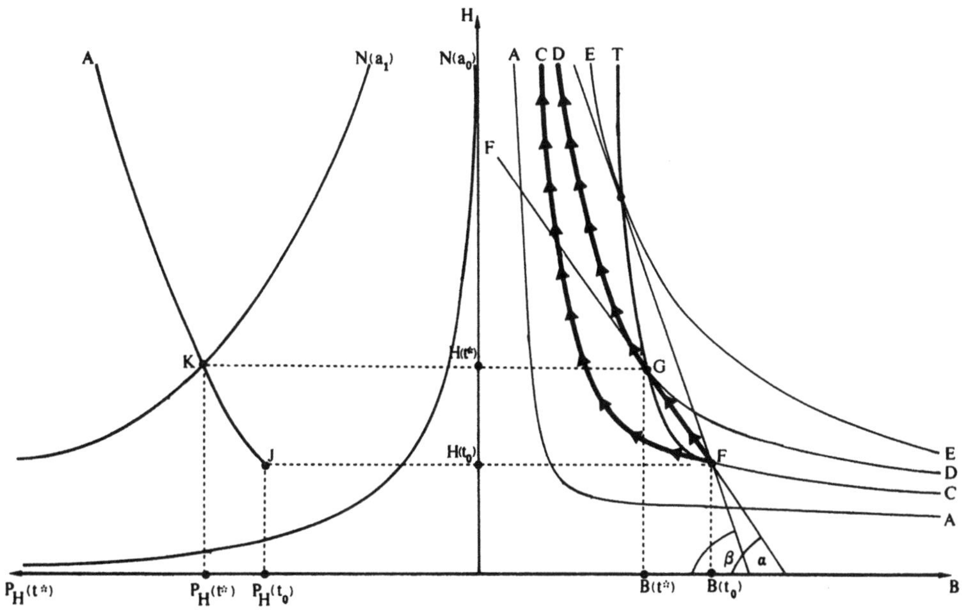

In real time housing stock and vacant land stock must move along one of these curves as long as investment in new housing units occurs. Which one of these hyperbolas is the relevant one depends upon the initial situation $[H(t_o), B(t_o)]$; in figure 6 this is hyperbola CC. Point F is the graphical starting point of the analysis.

If in the planning period t_o the marginal willingness to pay for land, $\frac{\beta}{\alpha}\varepsilon$, falls short of the desired land price, P_B, then, according to the previous reflections, there will be no land transactions during a transition period (t^*, t^{**}), implying $\hat{H} = 0$ in this period. Therefore, the system remains at point F during this period and moves along the curve CC beyond t^{**}, the direction of the movement indicated by arrows. The decreasing slope of the trajectory also provides information about the change in the marginal capital intensity of land over time. From (II.10) and (II.45) and because of $E = \alpha\delta H$ one derives

$$\text{(II.78)} \quad \frac{dH}{dB} = \frac{\dot{H}}{\dot{B}} = -\varphi(\varepsilon).$$

The steeper the equilibrium trajectory, i.e. the smaller the remaining stock of vacant land, the bigger are the houses built upon a building lot of given size.

But there is no guarantee that the system always evolves along the isoelastic path CC. If in the planning period t_o the marginal value product of land equals the desired price of land, there will be construction activities during the meta-time period (t_o, t^*) as well; this is shown in figure 4. Expressed in real time there is a discontinuous adjustment of the stocks H and B. To illustrate these jumps graphically we have to refer to equation (II.78) as well as to the determinants of the variable ε and their dynamic behaviour during (t_o, t^*). As is stated in condition (II.57), the landlord's choice of the marginal capital intensity is contingent on the price ratio P_B. And condition (II.59) states that this ratio does not change its value as long as the meta time runs. Therefore neither the marginal capital intensity nor the marginal structural density, $\varphi(\varepsilon)$, change their values during (t_o, t^*). Consequently, the common meta-time trajectory of the stocks H and B can be described by a negatively sloped straight line, starting in point F; this results from equation (II.78). In figure 6, the line FF illustrates the jump in the state variables H and B occuring in the planning period. The slope of FF is equal to the tangens of the angle α, with $\tan\alpha = -\varphi[\varepsilon_o(t_o)]$. Moreover, the duration of the meta-time period can be gathered from figure 6. Considering that in an optimal control problem the continuity of state variables and co-state variables is required, the meta-time period expires exactly at that point where the meta-time trajectory is tangential to another rectangular hyperbola. In the diagram of figure 6 point G is such a tangential point. Expressed in real time the system jumps from the initial state $[H(t_o),B(t_o)]$ into the state $[H(t^*),B(t^*)]$ and will evolve beyond t^* as is indicated by the path GD.

The graphical operation described above for a certain value of the marginal capital intensity of land, $\varepsilon_o(t_o)$, can be applied to the whole continuity of possible values for the variable ε [in figure 6 this is outlined for a value $\varepsilon_1(t_o) > \varepsilon_o(t_o)$, implying $\tan\beta = -\varphi[\varepsilon_1(t_o)] < \tan\alpha$]. If one derives for every possible value of ε the corresponding tangential point and depicts these points one finds the curve FT in the right quadrant of figure 6. This curve is the geometrical locus of all possible situations resulting from jumps in the state variables in the planning period t_o. In what follows, the curve FT will be referred to as <u>tangency curve</u>.

Which point on the tangency curve will be sighted by a ray emanating from point F depends on the price ratio $P_B(t_o)$; the value of this price ratio again depends on the landlord's marginal willingness to pay for land, which in its turn will be higher the more advantageous the current situation in the rental market. The correlation between the actual demand for housing services and the actual propensity to invest in new housing units is described in the left quadrant of figure 6. The abscissa represents the house price occurring in period $t^* (\equiv t_o)$. The curve A indicates the stock of housing units the landlord is willing to hold in t^* at different levels for $P_H(t^*)$. According to the homogeneity assumption made in section 2, the curve A can also be interpreted as the supply curve for housing services. This curve can be derived algebraically by noting that a movement up the tangency curve increases both the marginal structural density $\varphi[\varepsilon(t^*)]$ and the housing stock in which the initial building activity results. This allows for the formulation of the following functional relationship:

(II.79) $H(t^*) = \Phi[\varphi(\varepsilon(t^*))], \ \Phi' > 0.$

Substituting the inverse of efficiency condition (II.56) into (II.79) yields the desired relation between house price and optimal housing stock:

(II.80) $$H(t^*) = \Phi\{\varphi[\dot{\varphi}'^{-1}(1/P_H(t^*))]\}.$$

A straightforward calculation proves that $H(t^*)$ increases with $P_H(t^*)$, i.e.

(II.81) $$\frac{\partial H(t^*)}{\partial P_H(t^*)} > 0.$$

Equation (II.81) states that the higher the present value of rental receipts, the stronger the incentive for the landlord to provide (additional) housing services. As can be seen from figure 6, the supply curve has a lower bound, indicated by point J: owing to the assumptions that housing investment is irreversible and that the house price exceeds the cost of maintenance, the stock of housing units (the supply of housing services) cannot fall below its initial level $H(t_o)$. It is also worth noting that, given t^*, the functional relationship in (II.80) does not depend on t. The supply curve will not change its position when real time elapses, provided that there are no unanticipated changes in the planning data.

In figure 6 the optimal stock of housing units $H(t^*)$ is derived from the intersection point between the supply curve described above and a demand curve, labelled N, for housing services. This demand curve is an alternative version of the graph of optimality condition

(II.57) $$\hat{P}_H = -\frac{m(\frac{a}{H})}{P_H} + r + \alpha\delta.$$

Considering, that from (II.64) and (II.65) it follows

(II.82) $$\hat{P}_H = \beta\hat{P}_B,$$

equation (II.57) can be rearranged to

(II.83) $$P_H(t^*) = \frac{m[\frac{a(t)}{H(t)}]}{r+\alpha\delta-\beta\hat{P}_B} = \frac{m[\frac{a(t)}{H(t)}]}{(1-\beta)r+\alpha\delta}, \qquad \text{for all } t \geq t^*.$$

Equation (II.83) describes the marginal willingness of a potential house purchaser to pay for one unit of housing stock at different levels of this stock. And because P_H is directly related to the household's marginal willingness to pay, the curve N also provides information about the consumption behaviour of households. Holding parameter a constant and considering $m_H < 0$, it is easy to show that the slope of this curve has to be negative. Note that the demand curve has a stable position for a given point in time, but because of the growth in the parameter a it is gradually drifting to the left as real time goes by. Nevertheless, equation (83) defines the position of the demand curve uniquely for all $t > t^*$. It is particularly important to identify this position for the real-time starting point $t_o (\equiv t^*)$. The left quadrant of figure 6 features two fundamentally different cases:

- Suppose the demand curve $N(a_0)$ represents the demand situation prevailing in t_o, implying that the households are not willing to consume the existing supply of housing services at the going rental rate. Because of the irreversibility of housing investment the landlord has only two alternatives--to leave a part of his housing stock vacant or to rent out the whole housing stock at a lower, market-clearing rate. Facing these options his willingness to invest in new housing units is low. In particular he is not willing to pay the desired land price $P_B(t_o)$. Since the landowner in knowledge of the future demand for housing services on his turn will not agree on price cuts, this leads to a transitory suspension of construction activities. The transition period lasts until the demand function, pushed by the increase in the demand for housing services, touches the supply curve at the latter's lower end. In terms of figure 6 the equilibrium point rests for a while at F and will then gradually move along the curve FC;
- the demand curve $N(a_1)$ indicates a situation where initially the demand for housing services, given the rental rate, exceeds the current supply of this good. In this case it will be profitable for the landlord to increase his stock of housing services as fast as possible, since the marginal value product of land and the marginal value product of capital exceed the corresponding factor prices. Optimality conditions (II.56) and (II.57) will again be satisfied when the housing stock H has reached his optimal level $H(t^*)$. The adjustment from $H(t_o)$ to $H(t^*)$ takes place during the meta-time

period (t_o, t^*), whereby the system jumps to this point of the tangency curve FT whose H-co-ordinate is equal to $H(t^*)$. After t^* the economy moves along the hyperbola which is tangent to the path FF.

Figure 6 and the catalogue of optimality conditions hiding behind it provide the necessary tools to describe the reactions of housing and land markets to the imposition of various forms of taxation. In particular the meta-time period (t_o, t^*) and the transition period (t_1, t^{**}) become relevant if the planning problems discussed in this chapter are disturbed by unanticipated changes in the underlying informations.

To understand the mechanics of such reactions, it is sufficient to consult the following equations and the changes of these equations occurring in response to the introduction of single taxes:

$$\text{(II.77)} \quad \frac{dH}{dB} = \frac{H[\hat{a} - \eta\beta P_B]}{B[\hat{a}-(\eta\beta+\alpha)\hat{P}_B]} \quad ,$$

$$\text{(II.79)} \quad H(t^*) = \Phi\{\varphi[\varphi'^{-1}(1/P_H(t^*))]\},$$

$$\text{(II.83)} \quad P_H = \frac{m(\frac{a}{H})}{r + \alpha\delta - \beta\hat{P}_B} \ .$$

If the implementation of a single tax causes a change of the differential dH/dB in equation (II.77), a turn of the isoelastic curves and the tangency curve in figure 6 follows straightforwardly. Moreover, a tax-induced change in dH/dB also has an impact on the position of the supply curve described by equation (II.79): because of equation (II.78) the marginal condition (II.56) can be rewritten as

$$\text{(II.56)'} \quad P_H = 1/\varphi'(\varepsilon)$$

$$= 1/\varphi'[\varphi^{-1}(|dH/dB|)] \ ,$$

with $dP_H / d(|dH/dB|) > 0$. Equation (II.56)' produces a direct relationship between the slope of the rectangular hyperbolas in the right quadrant of figure 6 and the position of the supply curve in the left quadrant of this diagram. If the introduction of a tax results in an increase (decrease) of $|dH/dB|$, the supply curve will shift to the left (right).

A tax induced change of condition (II.56) can be illustrated by correspondent shifts of the supply curve. Note that this change has no impact on the position of the curve plotted in the right quadrant of figure 6.

Finally, tax induced changes of equilibrium condition (II.83) indicate shifts of the demand curve. It is also important to note that shifts in the demand curve and the supply curve explain the reaction of the model economy in the short run; the impact of taxation in the long run can be read from the tax-induced changes in the position of the isoelastic curves and the tangency curve in the right quadrant of figure 6.

III. Taxation and Market Reactions

After going through the details of the solution procedure we can now examine the effects of various forms of taxation. Because the trajectory of the laissez-faire economy is unique and Pareto-optimal, all tax-induced deviations from this path are equivalent to welfare losses. As mentioned above it is the substitution effects caused by taxation which are exclusively responsible for these inefficiencies. The substitution effects can be isolated from the also tax induced income effects by assuming that the public sector uses all the tax revenue to finance a lump-sum transfer program such that each household receives exactly that amount of money it paid in taxes.

According to the partial-equilibrium framework presented in chapter II, the interpretation of the results to be delivered by the succeeding analysis is restricted to a second-best level. We can make judgements about tax-induced intrasectoral distortions only as far as the housing sector, the building land sector, and the capital market are concerned. The remaining sectors of an economy usually also are subject to various forms of special tax treatment that defy a global evaluation. Moreover, tax distortions outside the sector of firms cannot be taken into account without further complications; one well-known example is the impact of income taxation on the work-leisure choice of private households.

Facing these limitations we will refer to a tax as being efficient if it contributes to a reduction of endogenous inefficiencies. A tax is referred to as being neutral if its imposition is free from endogenous substitution effects.

1. LAND TAXATION

1.1 A Tax On The Value Of Land

Both, the landlord and the landowner principally are subject to land taxation. It is important to note that in the context of current tax laws the term "land tax" is misleading. In most Western economies the imposition of land taxes is not necessarily restricted to the value of land exclusively. It is usually the market value of the whole property, including the value of any structures built upon the taxed item, that is subject to taxation. Let τ_L be the relevant tax-rate. Provided that the assessment of land property for tax purposes is up-to-date, the land-owner's tax liabilities are

$$T_L^{LO} = \tau_L P_B B, \tag{III.1}$$

whereas the landlord has to pay taxes by the amount of

$$T_L^{LL} = \tau_L P_H H \tag{III.2}$$

dollars.

As a matter of fact land taxes are not only levied because the government needs funds to finance its expenditures. Land taxes often are also used as a tool for regulating housing markets and land markets. By taxing vacant land at a higher effective rate than developed land the authorities intend to put a pressure on landowners to advance the developement of vacant land, which is supposed to cause falling land prices, an intensification of construction activities, and a more extensive provision of housing services. It will be interesting to examine whether the favourable tax treatment of developed land is an appropriate tool to realize the political goal of improving the housing standards of a society.

In order to be able to do this within the analytical framework provided in chapter II, the tax-function (III.2) has to be modified:

$$T_L^{LL} = \tau_L \rho_1 P_H H. \tag{III.3}$$

In equation (III.3) the parameter ρ_1 is allowed to adopt values between zero and one, $\rho_1 = 0$ indicating that developed land is not taxed at all and $\rho_1 = 1$ representing the case where developed land is taxed at the same rate as vacant land. In addition, $\rho_1 < 1$ states that developed land can be treated favourably either by charging a lower tax rate or by assessing a smaller than actual market value*).

---

*) Since only the differential tax-treatment of vacant and developed land is of interest it is reasonable to assume that vacant land is taxed according to its current market value.

1.1.1 The taxation of vacant land

To derive the reactions of the landowner and the landlord to the imposition of a tax on vacant land the tax function (III.1) has to be substituted into the laissez-faire decision problem (II.19). The landowner's goal now is to maximize the sum of present values of sale revenues net of tax. His decision problem therefore reads

$$\text{(III.4)}\quad \underset{\{F^s\}}{\text{Max}}\ M_B(t_o) \equiv \int_{t_o}^{\infty} [P_B(t)F^s(t) - z\tau_L P_B(t)B(t)]\exp[-zr(t-\min(t,t^*))]\,dt$$

under the constraints

$$\text{(II.1)}\quad B(t_o) > 0,$$

$$\text{(II.17a)}\quad z = \begin{cases} 0 & \text{for } t_o \leq t < t^* \\ 1 & \text{for } t \geq t^* \end{cases},$$

$$\text{(II.45)}\quad \dot{B} = -F^a .$$

Accordingly the Hamiltonian for this problem is

$$\text{(III.5)}\quad \mathcal{H} = P_B F^s - z\tau_L P_B B - \lambda_B F^s .$$

The partial derivatives of equation (III.5) with respect to the control variable F^s and the state variable B yield in addition with the canonical equation the optimality conditions for the equilibrium land-supply path:

$$\text{(III.6a)}\quad \hat{P}_B = 0 \qquad \text{for } t_o \leq t < t^*,$$

$$\text{(III.6b)}\quad \hat{P}_B = r + \tau_L \qquad \text{for } t \geq t^* .$$

As in the tax-free situation the land price remains constant during the meta-time period (t_o, t^*). But condition (III.6b) signals that the land price grows at a higher rate after t^* in response to the introduction of the tax. Obviously the landowner changes his plans by advancing the sale of vacant land in order to avoid a part of the tax, buying tax-free assets with the additional revenues. As a consequence of the altered sale plan the land price falls in the initial period. Moreover, the advance of sales leads to a shortage in the supply of vacant land in future periods. This can be established by substituting optimality condition (III.6b) into equation

$$(II.13)\quad \hat{F} = \hat{a} - \hat{P}_B(\eta\beta + \alpha) = \text{constant} < 0.$$

In the equilibrium with this tax, the volume of land transactions decreases at a higher rate than in the tax-free economy. Given the time path of land demand, this causes an increase in the growth rate of P_B. According to condition (III.6b) the new sale plan is optimal if the resulting growth rate of the land price is sufficient to cover <u>all</u> opportunity costs involved in the holding of vacant land, now also including the collectable tax. Because of the tax - induced increase in $\hat{P}_B$ and despite its initial drop, the land price will exceed its laissez-faire level after some finite point of time $\bar{t} > t^*$.

Whether the landlord is willing to cover this tax-induced increase in the opportunity cost of holding vacant land depends upon the demand for housing services. As can be shown, the parameter a must now grow at a higher rate than in the laissez-faire situation:

$$(III.7)\quad \hat{a} > \eta\beta(r + \tau_L).^{*)}$$

Only if condition (III.7) holds will the landlord be willing to pay the demanded land price beyond t^*. If condition (III.7) does not hold, the total stock of vacant land will be sold and built upon during the meta-time period (t_o, t^*). The landowner knows not only that the landlord will not pay the demanded land price but also that the difference between desired price and willlingness to pay will be the higher the further beyond t^* the sale is deferred.

For the purpose of this analysis it is more interesting to consider the case where condition (III.7) is satisfied. Since in this section developed land is assumed to be tax-free, the landlord's

---

*) Condition (III.7) can be derived from the general condition (II.67) $\hat{a} > \eta\beta\hat{P}_B$ by considering optimality condition (III.6b).

optimal behaviour can be described by referring to the laissez-faire optimality conditions

(III.8) $P_H \varphi'(\varepsilon) = 1,$ for $t \geq t_o$,

(III.9) $\frac{\beta}{\alpha}\varepsilon \{\substack{<\\=}\} P_B \Rightarrow F \{\substack{=\\>}\} 0$ for $t \geq t_o$,

(III.10a) $\hat{P}_H = 0$ for $t_o \leq t < t^*$,

(III.10b) $\hat{P}_H = -\frac{m}{P_H} + r + \alpha\delta$ for $t \geq t^*$.

Obviously the tax rate does not appear in the conditions above. But it would be wrong to conclude from this that the landlord's initial investment plans are not affected by the imposition of a tax on vacant land. Facing the initial drop in land prices, the landlord revises his decision concerning the capital intensity of land in favour of the usage of vacant land. In addition to a decrease in the capital intensity of land falling land prices also cause an overall decrease in the production cost of new housing units, inducing the landlord to increase his investment activities at least in the initial period t_o. Conditions (III.8) provide the formal confirmation for these reflections. The tax induced decrease of the parameter ε leads to a rise of the marginal product of construction services, $\varphi'(\varepsilon)$. Given that the price $P_I(=1)$ is constant, condition (III.8) can be satisfied only if the house price, or the rental rate, $m(\frac{a}{H})$, respectively, falls simultaneously.

Given the demand for housing services, this initial drop in $m(\frac{a}{H})$ can only be caused by an initial increase in the housing stock, H.

Moreover, the landlord knows that the landowner is able to shift a part of the tax burden by reducing the future land sales. His reaction to this is twofold: first, the capital intensity of land will rise faster over time than it would have risen in a tax free economy. This follows from equation (II.65) in connection with condition (III.6b). Second, the housing stock grows at a lower rate than its laissez-faire counterpart. This can be proven by substituting optimality condition (III.6b) into the general growth-equation

(II.71) $\hat{H} = \hat{a} - \eta\beta\hat{P}_B$.

Hence, despite of its initial increase, the housing stock will fall short of its laissez-faire level before long. The resulting reduction in the provision of housing services is the means that enables the landlord to shift at least a part of his tax burden to his tenants.

The tax induced acceleration in the growth of the rental rate is reflected in a faster growing house price. Considering the modified Hotelling rule in condition (III.6b), it follows from equation (II.64) that in the equilibrium with tax, the price P_H grows at the rate

$$\text{(III.11)} \quad \hat{P}_H = \beta(r + \tau_L).$$

The dynamic consequences of the imposition of a tax on vacant land are illustrated in figure 7. Referring to condition (III.6b) it can be shown that the slope of the hyperbolas in the right quadrant of figure 6 decreases in each point of the (H,B)-plane. The algebraic expression for this slope is

$$\text{(II.77)} \quad \frac{dH}{dB} = \frac{H[\hat{a} - \eta\beta\hat{P}_B]}{B[\hat{a} - (\eta\beta+\alpha)\hat{P}_B]} < 0.$$

Obviously, the differential $\frac{dH}{dB}$ decreases, measured in absolute values, if the parameter $\hat{P}_B$ rises owing to taxation. In figure 7 the path FC therefore pivots to the left. According to its construction, the tangency curve moves in the same direction. In section II it is shown that the supply curve in the left quadrant of figure 6 moves to the right if $|dH/dB|$ decreases. This shift reflects the landlord's willingness to increase his stock of housing units in response to the initial drop in land price.

Figure 7

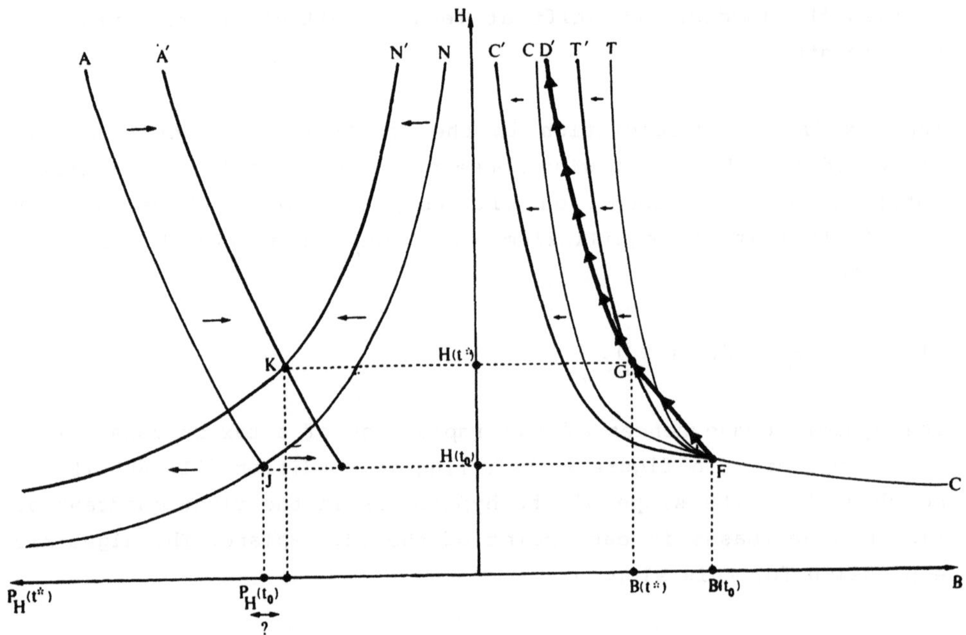

The introduction of the tax also affects the locus of the demand curve. Solving (III.10b) for P_H, using condition (III.6b), yields the equation for the after-tax demand curve:

$$P_H = \frac{m(\frac{a}{H})}{(1-\beta)r + \alpha\delta - \beta\tau_L} \qquad \text{(III.12)}$$

Equation (III.12) differs from its laissez-faire counterpart (II.82) by the tax term $\beta\tau_L$: the higher c.p. the tax rate, the bigger the ratio on the right side of equation (III.12) - and the higher the house price. As a consequence of taxing vacant land the demand curve shifts to the left in its new position N', reflecting that because developed land is assumed to be tax free it is the more desirable asset compared to vacant land.

The gap between the initial housing stock $H(t_o)$ and the new optimal housing stock $H(t^*)$ will be closed during the meta-time period (t_o, t^*). Initially falling land prices and the decreasing user cost of wealth tied into developed land thus induce a short-run construction boom in the housing market. After the end of meta time the economy evolves along the path GD. This path is characterized by the facts that

- the rental rate, m, the house price, P_H, and the land price, P_B, grow at a higher rate than in the tax-free economy. Therefore, despite their tax-induced initial drop all prices will exceed their laissez-faire level in finite time;
- the housing stock grows slower and the stock of vacant land shrinks slower than they did before the imposition of the tax. Therefore, the housing stock H will be less than its laissez-faire level after some infinite period of time.

1.1.2 The taxation of developed land

As stated earlier, the landlords tax liabilities amount to

$$\text{(III.13)} \quad T_L^{LL} = \tau_L \rho_1 P_H H.$$

The distributions A of a given period can be derived by subtracting from the gross rental revenues, mH, the net decrease in debt, -S, the expenditures for maintenance, E, the interest liabilities, rD, the expenses for the construction of new housing units, $F^d \varepsilon + P_B F^d$, and the tax payments, T_L^{LL}.

The formal description of the landlords decision problem is

$$\text{(III.14)} \quad \max_{\{S,E,\varepsilon,F^d\}} M_H(t_o) \equiv \int_{t_o}^{\infty} A(t)\exp[-zr(t-t^*)]dt$$

under the constraints

$$\text{(III.15)} \quad A = z(mH - E - rD - \tau_L \rho_1 P_H H) - F^d \varepsilon - P_B F^d + S,$$

and (II.2), (II.3), (II.9), (II.10), (II.14), (II.16), (II.17a). The corresponding Hamiltonian reads

$$\text{(III.16)} \quad \mathcal{H} = z(mH - E - rD - \tau_L \rho_1 P_H H) - F^d \varepsilon - P_B F^d + S$$

$$+ P_H [F^d \varphi(\varepsilon) - z(\alpha\delta H - E)]$$

$$+ \lambda_D D.$$

As can be shown easily by differentiating the Hamiltonian in (III.16) with respect to the controls S and E, the taxation of developed land does not affect the laissez-faire paths of financing and maintenance.

Differentiating the Hamiltonian with respect to the controls ε and F^d and the state variable H, considering the canonical equation for H, the following conditions can be achieved:

$$\text{(III.17)} \quad P_H \varphi'(\varepsilon) = 1 \qquad \text{for } t \geq t_o,$$

$$\text{(III.18)} \quad \frac{\beta}{\alpha}\varepsilon \left\{\substack{<\\=}\right\} P_B \Rightarrow F^d \left\{\substack{=\\\geq}\right\} 0 \qquad \text{for } t \geq t_o,$$

$$\text{(III.19a)} \quad \hat{P}_H = 0 \qquad \text{for } t_o \leq t < t^*,$$

$$\text{(III.19b)} \quad \hat{P}_H = -\frac{m}{P_H} + r + \alpha\delta + \tau_L \rho_1 \qquad \text{for } t \quad t \geq t^*.$$

The conditions (III.17) and (III.18) are well-known from the analysis of the laissez-faire economy. Condition (III.17) requires the equality of the marginal value product of construction services and the cost of the marginal service unit if the investment optimum is to be obtained. Condition (III.18) states that there will be construction activities ($F^d > 0$) only when the marginal value product of land ($\frac{\beta}{\alpha}\varepsilon$) equals the desired price for land. The case where the marginal value product exceeds the price P_B can be ruled out by referring to the existence condition for a solution to the landlord's planning problem. Both conditions also signal that the tax on developed land directly affects neither the decision concerning the marginal capital intensity of land nor the decision concerning the consumption of land. The tax is levied on the value of the whole property, which according to the technology in use is independent from the values of the factors of production. Moreover, conditions (III.17) and (III.18) imply that the tax on developed land has no impact on the growth characteristics of the model economy: the laissez-faire relationships

(III.20) $\hat{P}_H = \beta\hat{\varepsilon},$

and

(III.21) $\hat{\varepsilon} = \hat{P}_B$

still hold.

Condition (III.19b) is the only condition in which the land tax rate appears. From the analysis in chapter II we know this condition describes an intersectoral arbitrage equilibrium, requiring the equality of the net rate of return out of the housing stock and the user cost of capital tied into this stock. Condition (III.19b) states that the imposition of a tax on developed land causes an increase in the user cost, the scale of this increase depending on the degree of preferential tax treatment of developed land compared to vacant land. If there is no preferential treatment ($\rho_1 = 1$) the gross rate of return on the last dollar invested in housing stock, $m/P_H + \hat{P}_H$, has to cover not only the laissez-faire opportunity cost of housing investment but also the proportional tax. Hence, the tax on developed land turns out to have a negative impact on housing investment even in the short run - in contrary to a tax on vacant land, that helps the housing sector to a short-run construction boom.

1.1.3 The intertemporal incidence of a tax on the property of land

This section deals with a general land tax that boasts the two previously discussed taxes as integral parts. This tax is an approximation of the tax laws concerning the taxation of land valid in almost all industrialized nations of the Western World.

The differential incidence of a tax on vacant land only and a general land tax can be shown by substituting optimality condition (III.6b) into optimality condition (III.19b), whereby equations (III.20) and (III.21) have to be considered, and solving the obtained expression for P_H. This operation generates the function for the demand curves N', N" and N''' in figure 8:

$$\text{(III.22)} \quad P_H = \frac{m(a/H)}{(1-\beta)r + (\rho_1-\beta)\tau_L + \alpha\delta} \quad .$$

The comparison of equation (III.22) with equation (III.12) shows that the shift of the demand curve to the left illustrated in figure 7 is at least smaller when developed land is taxed in addition to vacant land. In the case where the favourable tax treatment of developed land is less distinct, i.e. where $\rho_1 > \beta$, the demand curve even shifts to the right.

However, the taxation of developed land has no impact on the locus of he supply curve or the position of the isoelastic curves and the tangency curve in figure 7. The shifts of these curves captured in figure 8 are caused by the reaction of the landowner to the imposition of a tax on vacant land.

As shown in figure 8, the short-run incidence of a tax on the property value of land is not clear cut. Three fundamentally different cases can be distinguished:

- first, consider the case where the tax treatment of developed land is sufficiently preferential to ensure either a shift of demand curve to the left or a shift of the demand curve to the right that is overcompensated by the tax induced rightward shift of the supply curve. This situation is represented by the demand curve N'. Because the tax-induced advantage of falling land prices accompanied by falling production costs for new housing units outweighs the tax-induced disadvantage of increasing user-cost, we will observe a short-run construction boom in the housing market;
- the demand curve N''' represents the case where the rise in the user cost of wealth tied up in developed land, i.e. the decrease in the rentability of housing investment, dominates the decrease in production cost. In this situation the landlord does not

Figure 8

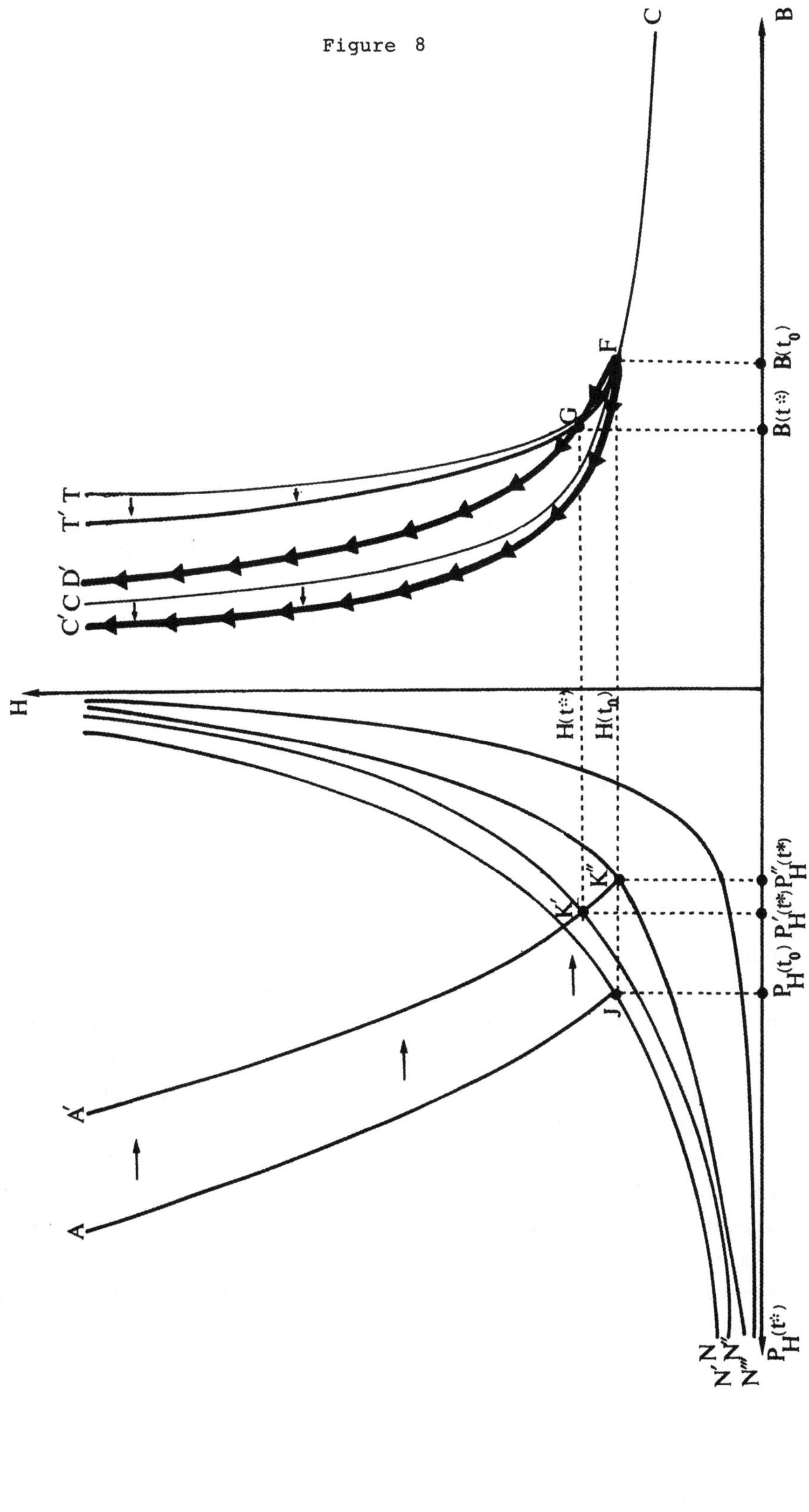

succeed in renting out his actual housing stock $H(t_o)$ at a cost-covering rate. His optimal strategy therefore is to postpone any construction activities until the households owing to the continual increase in rental demand are willing to pay this higher rent;

- also conceivable is the situation where after the adjustment of demand an supply plans the demand curve again touches the supply curve at its lower end. In this case neither a short-run construction boom nor a temporary halt in construction activities will take place.

While the short-run incidence of the land tax discussed in this section is ambigeous, its incidence is clear cut in the long run - as stated by equations (II.20) and (II.21) the tax on developed land has no impact on the model's growth rates. Referring to the reactions of landlord and landowner to the imposition of a tax on vacant land

- the stock of housing units grows at a lower rate than in the tax-free situation,
- the stock of vacant land and the consumption of vacant land both shrink at a higher constant rate,
- the rental rate, the per-unit price of housing stock, the price of vacant land and the marginal capital intensity grow faster than in the laissez-faire economy.

The results stated above provide some remarkable implications for policy issues. Apparently taxation based on the value of land property is a most inappropriate instrument to improve the housing quality (in our example measured in housing units) of a nation. Even in the short run and even if vacant land is discrinimated against the authorities cannot be sure that the expected construction boom takes place - unless they have detailed information about the technology in use (how big is β?). In the long run the tax is definitely counterproductive. Even in the case where the tax on land and development induces a short-run construction boom, the stock of housing units will fall short of its laissez-faire level in finite time. This results because the parameter H grows at a lower rate in the equilibrium with taxes, than in the tax-free world.

1.2 Site Value Taxation - The Best Solution?

As mentioned in the previous chapter, the term "land tax" can be misleading. The land tax levied in most Western economies in fact is a combination of

- a tax on the earning power of structures,
- and a tax on the site value of undeveloped land.

This conceptual difference in tax bases is the reason why frequently the land tax is said to be a source of discrimination: while owners of vacant land have to pay taxes only on the value of land, the owners of developed land have to pay taxes on both, the value of land and the value of the structure built on it. For this reason it is not surprising that in recent years there has been some interest in adopting site value as a tax base for developed land as well, excluding the value of structures. But there are different ideas about the way in which such a site value tax should be implemented. The disagreement essentially concerns the determination of the value of the structure's land share.

One suggestion is to value the share of land in the housing stock by the price P_B of vacant land. At least in the context of the model presented here, the impact of this proposition would be dramatic. Suppose that $B^*(t)$ stands for the share of land at a given point t of time, with $\dot{B}^*(t) = F(t)$. Then, the tax liabilities of the landlord in this period are

(III.23) $$T_L^{LL}(t) = \tau_L P_B(t) B^*(t).$$

In addition, the variable B^* would enter the landlord's decision problem as a state variable, requiring the transversality condition

(III.24) $$\lim_{t\to\infty} [P_B(t) B^*(t) e^{-r(t-t_o)}] = 0$$

to hold. Without (III.24) being fulfilled, the present value of the landlord's tax liabilities would be infinite and housing investment would not be profitable any longer. Condition (III.24) holds only if

(III.25) $$\hat{P}_B + \hat{B}^* - r = X < 0$$

also holds. In the previous section it is shown that in response to the imposition of a tax on vacant land the landowner readjusts his sale plans such that the resulting equilibrium growth rate of the land price is

(III.26) $\hat{P}_B = \tau_L + r.$

Substituting condition (III.26) into condition (III.25) and considering that (because of the irreversibility of housing investment) $\hat{B}^* \geq 0$ for all $t > t_o$, it can easily be shown that the parameter X in condition (III.25) is positive at each point of time, thus violating (III.24) and (III.25), respectively.

Using the tax base defined in equation (III.23) would virtually result in an expropriation of landlords. The economic intuition behind this conclusion is straightforward. Obviously the land price P_B is an arbitrary measure. To see this one has to consider the maximum net price the landlord could achieve by selling developed land on the market for vacant land. The realizable gross price certainly would be P_B. But the landlord also has to take into account the cost caused by the conversion of developed land into vacant land, i.e. forgone rental revenues and demolition cost. Only if the difference between gross price and conversion cost is non-negative the conversion will be a rational alternative. In the model introduced in chapter II demolition costs are assumed to be prohibitively high. Consequently it will be impossible in our model to find a market price for the land share of developed land. But even when the assumption of prohibitively high demolition costs is abandoned and the conversion of developed land into vacant land is taken into account, there is only one point of time in the history of an individual structure where it is possible to determine the value of its land share on ground of the price P_B: at the time of demolition this value is equal to the sum of land price and demolition cost. But as long as a conversion is not profitable an evaluation based on the calculus described above will necessarily yield wrong results.

What is the correct measure for the value of land's share in the housing stock H? Obviously there is no answer to this question. Because the construction technology is of the putty-clay type, an economic value can be assigned neither to the share of land nor to the structure built upon.

Nevertheless, since Ricardo presented his thoughts concerning the taxation of land, economists promote the imposition of a site value tax that is to be assessed on the rental value of land only, excluding the value of capital invested in this land. According to Ricardo such a tax is neutral.*)

In the context of our model, the revenue of a pure site value tax can be described by

$$\text{(III.27)} \quad T_L^{LL} = \tau_L (P_H H - K),$$

where $P_H H$ represents the market value of the housing stock H and K the value of capital invested. The state variable K follows the motion equation

$$\text{(III.28)} \quad \dot{K} = F^d \varepsilon - z(\delta K - E).$$

Using λ_K as the shadow value of the capital stock, the Hamiltonian for the landlord's decision problem is

$$\text{(III.29)} \quad \mathcal{H} = z[mH - E - rD - \tau_L (P_H H - K)] + S - F^d \varepsilon - P_B F^d$$
$$+ P_H [F^d \varphi(\varepsilon) - z(\alpha\delta H - E)]$$
$$+ \lambda_D S$$
$$+ \lambda_K [F^d \varepsilon - z(\delta K - E)].$$

Differentiating equation (III.29) with respect to the control variables ε and F^d and the state variables H and K, and considering that the tax treatment of the landowner under a site value tax would be the same as described in section III. 1.1., the following equilibrium conditions can be obtained:

*) Strictly speaking Ricardo referred to a tax on pure land rent. But because of the one-to-one relationship between land rent and land value, a tax on the value of land excluding the value of capital is equivalent to a tax on the pure rent, the tax rate τ_L defined as the product between the market interest rate and the tax rate assessed on pure rent.

$$(III.30)\quad P_H \varphi'(\varepsilon) = 1 - \lambda_K \qquad \text{for } t \geq t_o,$$

$$(III.31)\quad \frac{\beta}{\alpha}\varepsilon(1 - \lambda_K) \; \{\overset{<}{=}\} \; P_B \Rightarrow F \; \{\overset{=}{\geq}\} \; 0, \qquad \text{for } t \geq t_o,$$

$$(III.32)\quad \hat{P}_H = \hat{P}_B = 0 \qquad \text{for } t_o \leq t < t^*,$$

$$(III.33)\quad \hat{P}_H = - \frac{m}{P_H} + r + \alpha\delta + \tau_L \qquad \text{for } t \geq t^*,$$

$$(III.34)\quad \hat{P}_B = r + \tau_L \qquad \text{for } t \geq t^*,$$

$$(III.35)\quad \lambda_K = \frac{\tau_L}{r + \alpha\delta} .$$

According to condition (III.35) the shadow price λ_K reflects the fact that, given the present value of rental revenues, the market price of equity tied into the housing stock is higher the bigger the share of <u>tax free</u> construction services in stock H. Because the use of land as a factor of production is singled out for taxation, there is an incentive for the landlord to increase the capital intensity of his new housing investment, provided that the landowners are not willing to accept lower land prices. This statement is confirmed by conditions (III.30) and (III.31). From condition (III.33) it follows that the tax-induced increase in the user cost of housing property is the same as under the regime of the land tax discussed in section III.1.1 - as long as vacant land is not taxed at a higher effective rate (implying $\rho_1 = 1$). This result is not surprising: a site value tax of the type above is equivalent to a tax on the market value of the whole property combined with a governmental subsidy on the cost of construction services. Because of this equivalence, the differential incidence between a site value tax and a tax on the market value of the whole property is straightforward: a tax reform in favour of a site value tax would cause a short run construction boom, since the governmental subsidy not only reduces the relative cost of construction services compared to the cost of building land but also leads to a decrease in the overall production cost of new housing units. After the boom in the housing market has subsided, the further development of the economy can be described by the growth equations derived in the preceding section.

Figure 9 contains the graphical representation of the consequences of the switch from a land tax based on property value to a tax based on site value.

Figure 9

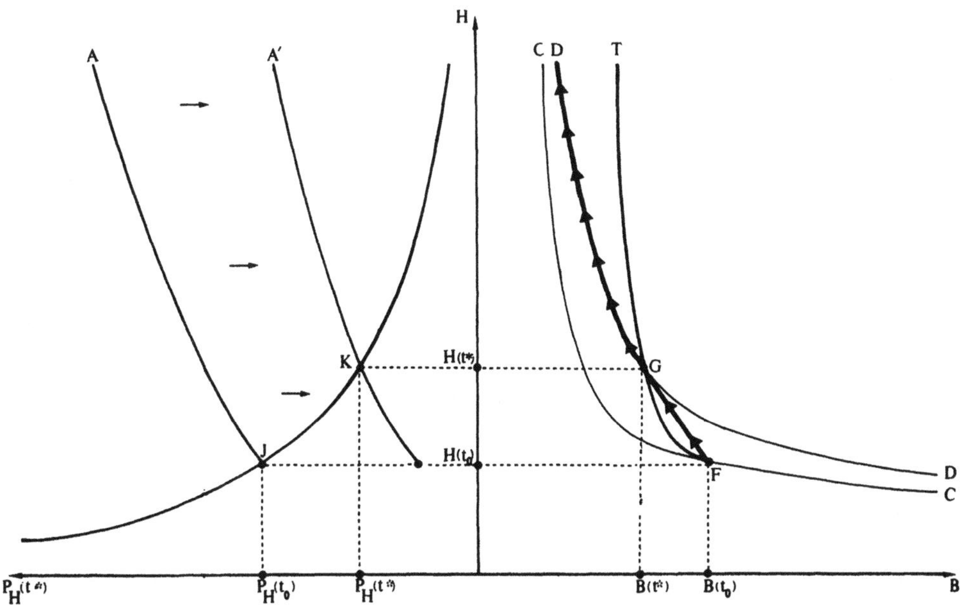

The differential incidence is expressed by the shift of the supply curve to the right. Referring to chapter II the supply of housing services in the planning period can be described by the general functional relationship

(II.79) $H(t^*) = \Phi\{\varphi[\varepsilon(t^*)]\}, \ \varphi', \ \Phi' > 0.$

Using the inverse of condition (III.30), equation (II.79) can be rewritten as

(III.36) $$H(t^*) = \Phi\{\varphi[\varphi'^{-1}(\frac{1-\lambda_K}{P_H(t^*)})]\},$$

with $\partial H(t^*)/\partial P_H(t^*)$, $\partial H(t^*)/\partial \lambda_K > 0$. With a glance on the signs of the partial derivatives, equation (III.36) states that at any given level of the housing stock $H(t^*)$ the house price $P_H(t^*)$ is smaller the bigger the shadow value λ_K, i.e. the shift of the supply curve is more distinct the higher the tax rate τ_L, all other things equal. Point K represents the optimum appearing after the introduction of the tax. According to point K the new optimal stock $H(t^*)$ exceeds the current stock $H(t_o)$. The necessary adjustment takes place during the meta-time period, where the system jumps from point F to point G in the right quadrant of figure 9. As a result of this temporary investment boom the rental rate $m(t^*)$ is lower and the land price $P_B(t^*)$ is higher than before the tax reform.

Since the tax reform has no impact on the growth rates derived in section III.1.1., the initial distortions affect the future periods as well: in each point of time $t \geq t^*$ the stock of housing units and the price of land are higher, and the stock of vacant land, the rental rate, and the house price are lower than they would have been without the amendment.

Obviously, a site value tax is everything but neutral. The landowner always has the option to reduce his tax liabilities by advancing the sale of vacant land. In addition, the landlord is able to avoid a part of the tax by increasing the capital intensity of land.

1.3 Neutral Taxation Of Land

1.3.1 The per-unit land tax

Faced with these results and the economic intuition behind them we have to ask whether there is any chance for a neutral taxation of land. After all, no one can forbid the landowner to by-pass the tax burden by selling the taxed item. In this context it is interesting to examine the incidence of a tax that according to the recent tax literature is also said to be neutral - the per-unit taxation of land. This tax is not imposed on the current value but on the area of land owned by landlords and landowners. Therefore, the tax to be paid by the landowner is

$$(III.37) \quad T_L^{LO} = \tau_L B,$$

with τ_L as the tax rate, whereas the landlord's tax liability is described by equation

$$(III.38) \quad T_L^{LL} = \tau_L B^*,$$

the parameter B^* representing the share of land included in the housing stock H. The variable B^* is a new state variable in the landlord's decision problem; the motion equation for B^* is

$$(III.39) \quad \dot{B}^* = F^d.$$

Substituting equations (III.37), (III.38) and (III.39) into the laissez-faire decision problems in chapter II, the corresponding Hamiltonians can be formulated as follows:

$$(III.40) \quad \mathcal{H}^{LL} = z(mH - E - rD - \tau_L B^*) + S - F^d \varepsilon - P_B F^d$$
$$+ P_H [F^d \varphi(\varepsilon) - z(\alpha\delta H - E)]$$
$$+ \lambda_D S$$
$$+ \lambda_{B*} F^d;$$

$$(III.41) \quad \mathcal{H}^{LO} = P_B F^s - \tau_L B - \lambda_B F^s.$$

In equation (III.40) the parameter λ_{B*} is used as shadow value for developed land; it is

$$\text{(III.42)} \quad \lambda_{B*} \equiv \frac{\partial M_H}{\partial B^*} = -\frac{\tau_L}{r}.$$

The shadow value signals by what amount the market value of the housing stock decreases, if - all other things being equal - the stock B^* increases by an incremental unit; λ_{B*} is the present value of all current and future tax liabilities caused by this marginal unit.

Differentiating the Hamiltonians in (III.40) and (III.41) with respect to the control and state variables and taking account of the canonical equations yields the optimality conditions

$$\text{(III.43)} \quad CF \sim EF \qquad \text{for } t \geq t_o,$$

$$\text{(III.44)} \quad E = \alpha\delta H \qquad \text{for } t \geq t^*,$$

$$\text{(III.45)} \quad P_H \varphi'(\varepsilon) = 1 \qquad \text{for } t \geq t_o,$$

$$\text{(III.46)} \quad \frac{\beta}{\alpha}\varepsilon \left\{\begin{matrix}<\\=\end{matrix}\right\} \bar{P}_B \Rightarrow F \left\{\begin{matrix}=\\ \geq\end{matrix}\right\} 0,\ \bar{P}_B = P_B - \frac{\tau_L}{r} \qquad \text{for } t \geq t_o,$$

$$\text{(III.47)} \quad \hat{P}_H = \hat{\bar{P}}_B = 0 \qquad \text{for } t_o \leq t < t^*,$$

$$\text{(III.48)} \quad \hat{P}_H = -\frac{m}{P_H} + r + \alpha\delta \qquad \text{for } t \geq t^*,$$

$$\text{(III.49)} \quad \hat{\bar{P}}_B = r \qquad \text{for } t \geq t^*.$$

Comparing conditions (III.43) - (III.49) with their laissez-faire counterparts, we see that the optimality conditions which appear under the regime of a per-unit land tax are the same as those achieved for the tax-free economy. Only the time path for the market price for vacant land has changed its level: as pointed out in condition (46), the new land price $\bar{P}_B$ is equal to the difference between the laissez-faire P_B and the present value of land taxes the landlord has to pay; or, to put it in another way, the landlord shifts his tax burden completely back to the landowner. Although the landowner in principle has the possibility to advance the sale of vacant land, there is no rational motive for him to do so. The only outcome of such a reaction would be a decrease in the present value of "before-tax" revenues, while the present value of his tax burden would remain unchanged. Because of this, a tax on land area, independent from value, is neutral.

1.3.2. A general tax on equity

An alternative way to tax wealth tied in land is used by some European countries. In West Germany, for example, a tax is levied on the value of all assets an individual taxpayer owns, including the equity tied in developed as well as in vacant land. In its ideal form and neglecting allowances the tax the landlord has to pay is based on the following value:

$$(III.50)\quad V^{LL} = P_H H - D;$$

In equation (III.50) the parameter D represents the stock of debt acquired in the past to finance housing investment; accordingly, the parameter V^{LL} symbolizes the market value of equity tied in the housing stock. The landowner's wealth subject to taxation is

$$(III.51)\quad V^{LO} = P_B B;$$

Using τ_V as tax rate and substituting the corresponding tax liabilities into the laissez-faire decision problems described in chapter II, the planning problem of the respresentative landlord and landowner can be rewritten in the following way: for the landlord we achieve

$$(III.52)\quad \max_{\{S,E,\varepsilon,F^d\}} M_H \equiv \int_{t_o}^{\infty} A(t)\exp[-z(r-\tau_V)(t-t^*)]dt$$

under the constraints (II.2), (II.3), (II.9), (II.10), (II.14), (II.16), (II.17a) and

$$(III.53)\quad A = z[mH - E - rD - \tau_V(P_H H - D)] + S - F^d\varepsilon - P_B F^d,$$

whereas for the landowner we have to solve the problem

(III.54) $$\max_{\{F^s\}} M_B \equiv \int_{t_o}^{\infty} (P_B F^a - z\tau_v P_B B)\exp[-z(r-\tau_v)(t-t^*)]dt$$

under the constraints (II.1), (II.17a) and (II.45).

In equations (III.53) and (III.54) the real interest rate net of tax, $r^* = r - \tau_v$, is used as factor of discount. This is done because it has to be considered that the market value of bonds and shares also is subject to taxation.

Differentiating the Hamiltonians corresponding to equations(III.53) and (III.54) with respect to the control and state variables, we obtain the following set of necessary conditions:

(III.55) $EF \sim CF$ for $t \geq t_o$,

(III.56) $E = \alpha\delta H$ for $t \geq t^*$,

(III.57) $P_H \varphi'(\varepsilon) = 1$ for $t \geq t_o$,

(III.58) $\frac{\beta}{\alpha}\varepsilon \left\{\begin{smallmatrix}<\\=\end{smallmatrix}\right\} P_B \Rightarrow F \left\{\begin{smallmatrix}=\\\geq\end{smallmatrix}\right\} 0$ for $t \geq t_o$,

(III.59) $\hat{P}_H = \hat{P}_B = 0$ for $t_o \leq t < t^*$,

(III.60) $\hat{P}_H = -\frac{m}{P_H} + r + \alpha\delta$ for $t \geq t^*$,

(III.61b) $\hat{P}_B = r$ for $t \geq t^*$.

The comparison of conditions (II.55) - (II.61b) with the equivalent laissez-faire conditions shows that at least within the partial-equilibrium framework of our analysis <u>the general tax on equity is neutral</u> not only with respect to the investment decision but also with respect to the financing decision.

In particular, the result concerning the optimal financing behaviour of the landlord might surprise. But despite the fact that the tax the landlord has to pay on the equity tied in the housing stock decreases when his indebtedness, all other things equal, increases, a change in the financing structure of the existing housing stock in favour of credit financing would not affect his total wealth: he has to pay tax on equity tied in houses as well as on equity tied in any other investment alternative.

For the same reason the tax does not affect his laissez-faire investment plan, nor does it affect the landowner's laissez-faire sale plan. Both agents realize that they are not able to reduce the present value of their tax payments by foregoing housing investment or advancing the sale of vacant land, respectively; they would have to pay an equal amount of taxes on every asset they could purchase with the released equity.

However, it is important to note that the neutrality result derived above is only valid in reference to the second-best criterion defined on page 54 . While the tax is neutral in an intersectoral context, it is not neutral if intertemporal efficiency is taken into account. The tax on equity obviously drives a wedge between the household's rate of time preference and the marginal efficiency of wealth. The imposition of a tax on equity causes a reduction of the opportunity cost of dissaving, implying that in the after-tax equilibrium the household's rate of time preference is equal to the market interest rate <u>net of tax</u>, $r - \tau_v$. The condition for an intersectoral arbitrage equilibrium, however, remains unaffected by the tax - the net rate of return out of housing investment still has to be equal to the <u>gross</u> market interest rate. Compared to the tax free situation, the imposition of an equity-tax hampers the accumulation of capital, thereby violating the condition for an intertemporal Pareto-optimum.

Moreover, the imposition of an equity tax is necessarily restricted to assessable assets; consequently, assets like human capital are tax exempt. From this it is plausible to conclude that households will adjust their portfolio in favour of these tax-free assets, for example extending their period of education and training to the debit of their life-time labor supply.

2. SALES TAXES AND VALUE ADDED TAXES

Even a shallow inspection of the tax laws of most countries in the industrialized world will show that there are considerable differences in the tax treatment of sale revenues achievable on different levels of the production and consumption processes in these economies. Canada, for example, is one of the few countries with a (federal) sales tax on manufacturers alone. While the United States forego the imposition of a (federal) sales tax completely, most of the European countries prefer a tax akin to a value added tax. Moreover, the comparison between North American an European tax regulations is complicated by the fact that specific retail sales taxes may be applied on a state or local level (U.S.A.) or on a provincial level (Canada). The following statements therefore refer only to the most distinct features of the different tax systems mentioned above.

2.1 Manufacturer Sales Tax (MST)

The base for the MST is the selling price of all goods manufactured or produced in Canada or imported into Canada unless specifically exempted*. In particular building material is subject to taxation. Building land, however, is tax exempt. Using τ_m as the symbol for the relevant tax rate, the price for a single unit construction service is

$$(III.62)\quad P_I = 1 + \tau_m .$$

Substituting this new price in the landlord's laissez-faire decision problem and differentiating the modified Hamiltonian with respect to the control and state variables yields the following optimality conditions:

---

* See Boadway and Kitchen (1984), pp. 259.

$$\text{(III.63)} \quad P_H \varphi'(\varepsilon) = 1 + \tau_m \qquad \text{for } t \geq t_o,$$

$$\text{(III.64)} \quad \frac{\beta}{\alpha}\varepsilon\,(1 + \tau_m) \left\{\begin{smallmatrix} < \\ = \end{smallmatrix}\right\} P_B \Rightarrow F^d \left\{\begin{smallmatrix} = \\ \geq \end{smallmatrix}\right\} 0 \qquad \text{for } t \geq t_o,$$

$$\text{(III.65)} \quad \hat{P}_H = 0 \qquad \text{for } t_o \leq t < t^*,$$

$$\text{(III.66)} \quad \hat{P}_H = -\frac{m}{P_m} + r + \alpha\delta \qquad \text{for } t \geq t^*.$$

As is stated by optimality conditions (III.63) and (III.64), the manufacturer's sales tax induces the landlord to change his plans concerning the optimal capital intensity of land as well as the volume of new housing investment. Because the sale of vacant land is exempted from the MST, it is profitable for the landlord to adjust the combination of inputs in favour of land. However, the assumed properties of the production function prevent the landlord from dodging the tax-induced increase in construction cost entirely by preferring the cheaper input. Therefore he also will reduce his initial investment plans at the time the tax is introduced. This last conclusion can be proven by referring to the general equation for the supply curve. Substituting the inverse of condition (III.63) into the supply function (II.79), the relationship between the house price and the stock of housing units in the planning period can be rewritten as

$$\text{(III.67)} \quad H(t^*) = \Phi\{\varphi[\varphi^{-1}(\frac{1+\tau_m}{P_H(t^*)})]\} .$$

Because of $\partial H(t^*)/\partial\tau_m < 0$, equation (III.67) states that for any initial level of $P_H(t^*)$ the initially optimal stock of housing units is smaller the higher the tax rate τ_m. Therefore, the landlord's response to the introduction of a MST can be illustrated graphically by a shift of the supply curve to the left. This is done in figure 10.

---

*) Obviously, the effective value of τ_m varies with the degree of vertical integration of production stages. In our analysis it is assumed that there is only one stage of production.

Figure 10

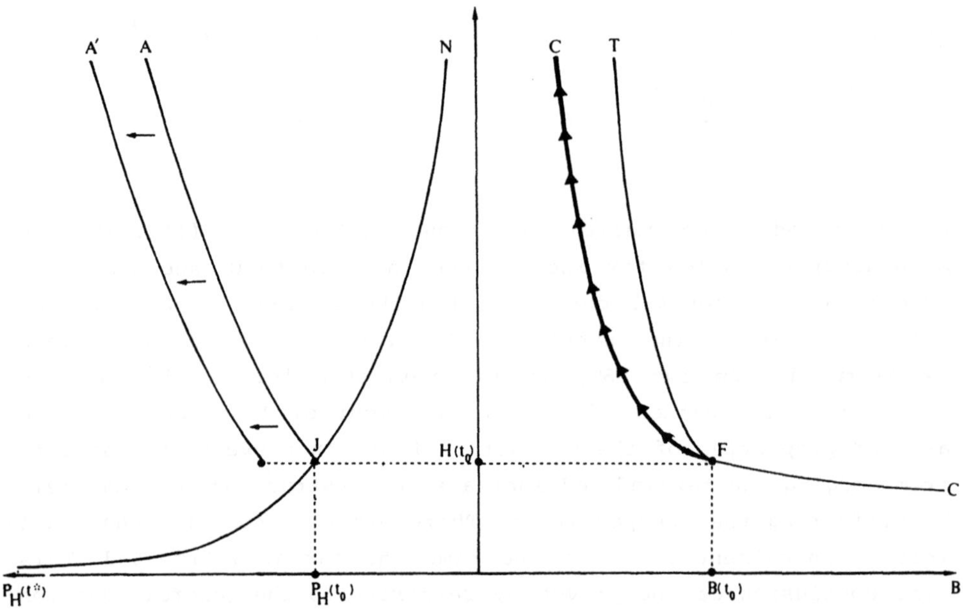

Figure 10 also includes the dynamic impacts of a tax on manufacturers' revenues. Because the going rental rate is insufficient to cover the cost of producing new rental accomodation there will be a temporary halt in construction activities. During this transition period the rent and the house price grow at their maximum rate. Construction activities will be resumed after the demand curve shifted so far to the left that it touches the supply curve at the latter's lower end. Because the MFT leaves the equilibrium growth rates of the model variables unaffected, the stock of housing units will fall short of its laissez-faire level in every point of time after the introduction of the tax. The stock of vacant land, the rental rate, and the house price, however, are higher for all $t > t_o$ than they would have been in a world without a MFT.

2.2 Retail Sales Tax (RST)

The retail sales tax, as far as it is imposed, applies to the selling price of goods sold for final use or consumption - unless specifically exempted by law. In Canada rental revenues are generally not subject to taxation, whereas in several states of the U.S. a tax on such revenues is levied. The imputed rents out of owner occupation, however, are tax exempt in both countries. In order to examine the effects of this preferential treatment of housing services compared to other consumption goods we have to leave the partial equilibrium framework of the analysis. In doing so tax induced distortions in the consumption plans of households can be considered. One of the basic results of consumer theory is that households look only on relative gross prices in order to determine their utility maximizing consumption bundle. Because the relative price of housing services decreases as a result of the tax exemption of rental revenues, households readjust their consumption plans in favour of these services.

In terms of our graphical analysis this tax induced change in consumption behaviour causes a shift of the demand curve to the left.

Figure 11

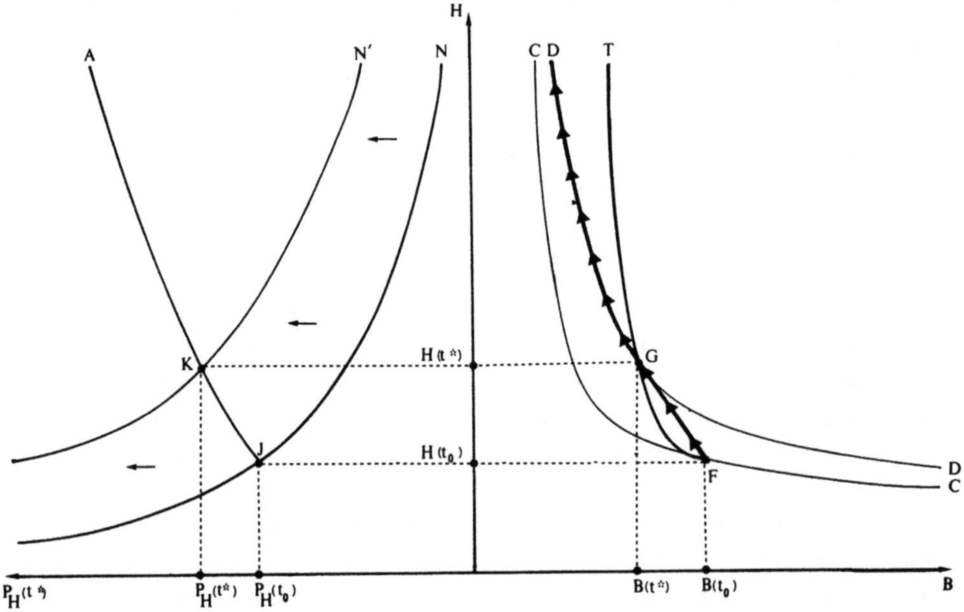

As a result of this demand distortion the profitability of housing investment increases. It can be read from figure 11 that the landlord reacts to this increase in rentability with an intensification of construction activities: the tax exemption of rental revenues helps the housing market to a short-run construction boom at the end of which the rental rate, the house price, and the price of vacant land are higher compared to the tax-free situation. Since the imposition of a RST has no impact on the economy's growth characteristics these initial distortions are carried forward to future periods. In every period beyond t_o the housing stock, the rental rate, the house price, the land price, and the consumption of vacant land, will exceed their corresponding laissez-faire levels, whereas the stock of vacant land will be smaller than in the tax-free situation.

2.3 Value Added Tax (VAT)

A VAT in its ideal form is neutral. In order to prove this statement it is not necessary to introduce the tax explicitly in the landlord's and landowner's optimization problems. The prices contained in the laissez-faire optimality conditions rather can be interpreted as prices net of tax. The economic intuition behind this neutrality result can be explained by referring to Brown's well known paper about the neutrality of a profit-tax*). As Brown pointed out, an income tax is neutral when the tax base is defined as the difference between the market value of the individual firm's output and gross investment expenditures incurred in a given period. This difference is the monetary equivalent of the value added generated by the taxed firm. With respect to our model, for a VAT to be neutral therefore requires a tax base, VA, defined in the following way:

$$\text{(III.68)} \quad VA = mH - P_B F^d - F^d \varepsilon - E .$$

The tax base for VATs imposed in most countries of Western Europe are not consistent with the ideal definition provided by equation (III.68). Usually they deviate from (III.68) in two significant details:

- First, while construction services are tax free, a similar exemption for building land does not exist. As can be shown by referring to the laissez-faire optimality conditions (II.56) and (II.57), this deviation has no impact on the landlord's investment plans:

---

*) See Brown (1948)

$$\text{(II.56)} \quad P_H \varphi'(\varepsilon) = 1 \qquad \text{for } t > t_o,$$

$$\text{(II.57)} \quad \frac{\beta}{\alpha}\varepsilon \left\{ \begin{matrix} < \\ = \end{matrix} \right\} P_B \Rightarrow F \left\{ \begin{matrix} = \\ \geq \end{matrix} \right\} 0 \qquad \text{for } t > t_o.$$

Both conditions also describe the equilibrium prevailing under the regime of an "imperfect" VAT of the type described above. The difference is that in the situation where an "imperfect" VAT is imposed the left sides of conditions (II.56) and (II.57) must be interpreted in values net of tax. Since expenditures for building land are not tax deductible, the marginal value product of land in the equilibrium with tax is the same as in the tax-free situation only if the price of building land after the imposition of the tax is $1/(1+\tau_{VA})$ times higher as the laissez-faire price P_B, τ_{VA} being the tax rate assessed on the "value added" in the housing sector. The "imperfect" VAT is neutral because the landlord is able to shift the tax burden back to the landowner.*)

In the first instance it might be surprising to learn that the landowner does not react to the landlord's attempt to shift the burden of the tax. The reason he maintains his initial sale plan becomes apparent if we interpret the shift as a tax the landlord imposes on the landowner. The tax rate is τ_{VA}, the tax base the value of vacant land, $P_B F$, used up for building purposes in a given period. Because of the Hotelling-rule derived in section II, the tax base grows at a rate equal to the discount rate, r. Therefore the present value of tax payments is the same independently of when the landlord chooses to sell a given area of vacant land.
Consequently he could reduce his tax burden (measured in present values) neither by postponing nor by advancing his land sales;

- second, rental revenues are tax exempt; if, as for example in Germany, this tax exemption implies that expenditures for gross investment $(F^d \varepsilon + E + P_B F^d)$ are <u>included</u> in the tax base of the

---

*) In section II it is shown that the optimal trajectory is unique. The equilibrium described above therefore is the only possible one.

"VAT", this preferential treatment of housing services has no direct influence on the landlord's investment plans. This statement follows immediately from the neutrality property of the VAT. However, the preferential treatment of housing services induces households to alter their consumption behaviour in favour of housing services. For this reason the effects of an "imperfect" VAT are equivalent to those of an RST described in the preceding section.

3. TAXATION OF INCOME FROM REAL ESTATE PROPERTY

3.1 A Neutral Income Tax

Before examining existing tax laws it is reasonable to provide the proof that a neutral income taxation of the housing sector and the affiliated building land sector is conceivable. The criticism that the demand for a more efficient income taxation is unrealistic, since unfeasible, can be avoided by referring to this ideal. Moreover, the ideal provides a helpful pattern for the modelling of proposals on how to improve existing income tax laws.

There is wide consent among economists that comprehensive income - suitably defined and with suitable deductions and exemptions - is the appropriate base for the taxation of individuals, both on horizontal and on vertical equity grounds. It will be shown in the following that such a comprehensive income tax also meets the neutrality requirements defined in the introductory part of Chapter III.*)

In the context of our model the landlord's comprehensive income tax base needs to

- include rental revenues; it makes no difference whether these rental revenues are the result of renting or of owner-occupation. In the case of renting the landlord receives the revenues from his tenants, in the case of owner-occupation he pays to himself.

---

*) The concept of a comprehensive income tax was first formulated by Schanz (1896); Haig (1921) and Simons (1938) promoted it in the English speaking areas.

- include all capital gains <u>accrued</u> in the housing stock, $\dot{P}_H H$, during the taxation period.

- exclude the amount of revenue necessary to serve outstanding mortgages, rD; these interest payments do not represent income, but costs caused by the attempt to increase or maintain the income flow.

- exclude all capital losses; in our model, capital losses are caused by the deterioration of housing capital included in the housing stock. As a result of deterioration, in any given period $\alpha\delta H$ housing units are eliminated from the stock H. Evaluating this quantity with the price P_H per housing unit yields the deterioration-induced capital loss, $P_H \alpha\delta H$.

According to these requirements, the landlord's tax liabilities are:

$$(III.68) \quad T_I^{LL} = \tau_I (mH + \dot{P}_H H - P_H \alpha\delta H - rD).$$

In equation (III.68) τ_I is used as income tax rate; for simplicity τ_I is assumed to be constant.

The definition of the landowner's tax base, consistent with the requirements of a comprehensive income tax, is relatively simple: neither has he to pay interest on debt - this is excluded by assumption - nor has he to consider deterioration-induced losses of his stock of vacant land. His only source of income are capital gains accrued in the stock B. Using $\dot{P}_B$ as the change of the land price in a given period, the landowner's tax liabilities are

$$(III.69) \quad T_I^{LO} = \tau_I \dot{P}_B B.$$

In order to determine the reactions of landlord and landowner to the imposition of a comprehensive income tax, equations (III.68) and (III.69) must be substituted into the corresponding laissez-faire decision problems (II.19) and (II.46).

The landowner's decision problem now reads

$$\text{(III.90)} \quad \underset{\{F^S\}}{\text{Max}}\ M_B(t_o) \equiv \int_{t_o}^{\infty} \{P_B(t)F^s(t) - z\tau_I \dot{P}_B(t)B(t)\} \exp[-z(1-\tau_I)r(t-t^*)]dt.$$

under the constraints

$$\text{(II.1)} \quad B(t_o) > 0,$$

$$\text{(II.17a)} \quad z = \begin{cases} 0 \text{ for } t_o \leq t < t^* \\ 1 \text{ for } t \geq t^* \end{cases},$$

$$\text{(II.45)} \quad \dot{B} = -F^s.$$

In equation (III.90) the market interest rate net of tax is used as discount rate, indicating that interest earned by alternative financial investment also is subject to taxation.

Similarly, the landlord's decision problem can be described as follows:

$$\text{(III.91)} \quad \underset{\{S,E,\varepsilon,F^d\}}{\text{Max}} \quad M_H \equiv \int_{t_o}^{\infty} A(t)\exp[-z(1-\tau_I)r(t-t^*)]\,dt$$

under the constraints

$$\text{(III.92)} \quad A = z(1-\tau_I)(mH-rD) - z(E - \tau_I\dot{P}_H H + \tau_I P_H \alpha\delta H) + S - F^d\varepsilon - P_B F^d,$$

$$\text{(II.2)} \quad H(t_o) > 0,$$

$$\text{(II.3)} \quad D(t_o) \gtrless 0,$$

$$\text{(II.9)} \quad 0 \leq E \leq \alpha\delta H,$$

$$\text{(II.10)} \quad \dot{H} = F^d\varphi(\varepsilon) - z(\alpha\delta H - E),$$

$$\text{(II.14)} \quad S \leq P_H[F^d\varphi(\varepsilon) - z(\alpha\delta H - E)] + \dot{P}_H H,$$

$$\text{(II.16)} \quad \dot{D} = S,$$

$$\text{(II.17a)} \quad z = \begin{cases} 0 \text{ for } t_o \leq t < t^* \\ \\ 1 \text{ for } t \geq t^* \end{cases} .$$

In the landlord's decision problem, too, the market interst rate net of tax is applied as discount rate.

Formulating the Hamiltonians corresponding to (III.90) and (III.91) and differentiating them with respect to the various control and state variables, and considering the canonical equations, the following optimality conditions can be achieved:

$$\text{(III.93)} \quad EF \sim CF \qquad \text{for } t \geq t^*,$$

$$\text{(III.94)} \quad E = \alpha\delta H \qquad \text{for } t \geq t^*,$$

$$\text{(III.95)} \quad P_H \varphi'(\varepsilon) = 1 \qquad \text{for } t \geq t_o,$$

$$\text{(III.96)} \quad \frac{\beta}{\alpha}\varepsilon \left\{\begin{smallmatrix}<\\=\end{smallmatrix}\right\} P_B \Rightarrow F\left\{\begin{smallmatrix}=\\ \geq\end{smallmatrix}\right\} 0 \qquad \text{for } t \geq t_o,$$

$$\text{(III.97)} \quad \hat{P}_H = \hat{P}_B = 0 \qquad \text{for } t_o \leq t < t^*,$$

$$\text{(III.98)} \quad \hat{P}_B = r \qquad \text{for } t \geq t^*,$$

$$\text{(III.99)} \quad \hat{P}_H = -\frac{m}{P_H} + r + \alpha\delta. \qquad \text{for } t \geq t^*.$$

The comparison of the laissez-faire optimality conditions with conditions (III.93)-(III.99) provides the formal confirmation that a comprehensive income tax satisfies the neutrality criterion defined at the beginning of chapter III . The landowner realizes that, although he is able to avoid the tax on capital gains by advancing the sale of vacant land i.e. rearranging the structure of his portfolio, there is no chance to avoid or reduce his income tax liabilities by doing so; in equilibrium the tax he would have to pay on income earned by alternative assets is exactly the same as the tax he has to pay due to the actual appreciation of the stock B.

Similarly, the landlord's plans - with respect to financing as well as to new construction and maintenance - are not affected by the imposition of the tax. The landlord remains indifferent with respect to the financing alternatives open to him because he realizes that the cost of every dollar equity invested in the housing stock, i.e. interest forgone by the amount of $r(1 - \tau_I)$ dollars, coincides with the effective cost of every dollar loaned, considering that interest payments are tax deductible. His maintenance plans remain unchanged because the imposition of the tax has an influence neither on the house price nor on the cost of maintenance activities. The laissez-faire decision about the construction of new housing units is not revised because the income tax is imposed on every kind of income - especially on income earned by assets that could be purchased as a result of foregoing housing investment - and because in equilibrium every kind of asset on the margin yields the same return.

3.2 The Ideal And Reality - Existing Income Tax Regulations

Current income tax regulations concerning income out of real estate property can touch the ideal defined in (III.68) and (III.69) not in the least. A first reason for the failure of evenly taxing housing income is that tax authorities usually distinguish between income earned by corporations and income earned by non-corporate firms. In the United States, for example, corporate income is taxed twice - on the corporate level and on the level of the individual shareholder - whereas non-corporate income is subject to taxation only on the personal stage. Nevertheless, in the framework of our analysis it is unnecessary to analyze the consequences arising from the double taxation of corporate income: the firm is able to dodge the disadvantage of double taxation by preferring debt financing instead of equity financing (the latter including the financing with both, retained earnings and the issue if new shares). For this reason we will concentrate in the following on the taxation of non-corporate income.

A second and more important reason for the inefficiency of current income tax regulations is that the definition of the income tax base in each case differs significantly from the ideals defined in (III.68) and (III.69). Moreover, housing income usually is treated differently, depending on whether it is the result of renting or of owner-occupation.

3.2.1 Income taxation of the landowner

a) The Tax Exemption of Capital Gains and the Phenomenon of "Land Speculation"

The appreciation of his stock of vacant land is the landowner's only source of income. But in most Western economies tax authorities exercise some remarkable discretion when concerned with the taxation of this kind of income. In not a single country are capital gains taxed on an accrual basis. And where a tax on realization is imposed, for example in Canada or in the United States, realized capital gains have to exceed a certain tax-exempt amount before they are subject to taxation. This allowance is the reason for that the taxation of capital gains is the exception rather than the rule.

First of all from an efficiency point of view, one is tempted to believe that this virtual tax exemption of realized capital gains causes no problems, since the landowner is treated in the same way as in the tax-free world. That he nevertheless changes his laissez-faire sale plans can be proved by taking into account that all other interest-bearing assets are subject to taxation. This fact can be reflected formally by using the net interest rate $(1 - \tau_I)r$ as factor of discount. The market value of the stock of vacant land in t_o then is

$$\text{(III.100)} \quad M_B(t_o) \equiv \int_{t_o}^{\infty} P_B(t)F^S(t)\exp[-z(1-\tau_1)r(t-t^*)]dt.$$

Again the landlord chooses that time path of land transactions that maximizes the market value defined in (III.100). Applying the familiar formal steps we achieve as necessary conditions for the optimal path of land sales:

$$(III.101a) \quad \hat{P}_B = 0 \qquad \text{for } t_o \leq t < t^*,$$

$$(III.101b) \quad \hat{P}_B = (1 - \tau_I)r \qquad \text{for } t \geq t^*.$$

Condition (III.101b) states that in an economy that foregoes the taxation of realized capital gains completely, the equilibrium growth rate of the land price is smaller than in a world where a comprehensive income tax is imposed. Consequently, the time path of land sales must differ from its laissez-faire counterpart. Because of the preferential tax treatment of the interest-bearing asset vacant land, there is an incentive for the individual household to adjust his portfolio in favour of this asset. As a result the landowner will reduce his supply of vacant land in the planning period t_o, causing an increase in the price of land in this period. Moreover, as time elapses, the stock of vacant land shrinks at a smaller rate than in the tax-free situation. This can be established by substituting the new after-tax equilibrium growth rate into the general equation (II.76). This operation yields

$$(III.102) \quad \hat{B} = \hat{a} - (1 - \tau_I)r(\eta\beta+\alpha) = \text{constant} < 0.$$

Hence, in every point of time after the imposition of an income tax featuring the special characteristics discussed in this section the stock of vacant land will exceed its laissez-faire level.

However, the reduction of the supply of land in the initial period implies that beyond t_o the supply of land must shrink at a lower rate than in the tax-free world. The formal confirmation of this statement can be achieved by referring to the general equation (II.74) and considering optimality condition (III.101b). The new equation for the time path of land supply therefore is:

$$(III.103) \quad \hat{F} = \hat{a} - (1 - \tau_I)r(\eta\beta+\alpha) = \text{constant} < 0.$$

Since the time path of demand for vacant land is given, this tax-induced change in sale plans causes the deceleration in the growth of the land price stated in equation (III.101b).

The landowner's reaction to the income tax exemption of capital gains accrued in the stock of vacant land can be illustrated graphically by a turn of the isoelastic hyperbolas in the right quadrant of figure 6. As shown in Chapter II, the slope of these hyperbolas is

$$(II.77)\quad \frac{dH}{dB} = \frac{H[\hat{a}-\eta\beta\hat{P}_B]}{B[\hat{a}-(\eta\beta+\dot{\alpha})\hat{P}_B]} < 0.$$

According to equation (II.77), using condition (III.101b), the slope of the hyperbolas gets steeper in every point of the (H,B)-plane. That the tangency curve also pivots around point F into its new position FT' follows straightforwardly from the construction of this curve.

The tax-induced changes in the landowner's sale plans also affect the landlord's investment plans. If we proceed on the assumption that the landlord's income is liable to taxation as described in section 3.1 of this chapter, his optimal investment decision is contingent to the equilibrium conditions:

$$(III.104)\quad P_H\varphi'(\varepsilon) = 1 \qquad \text{for } t \geq t_o,$$

$$(III.105)\quad \frac{\beta}{\alpha}\varepsilon \left\{\begin{matrix}<\\=\end{matrix}\right\} P_B \Rightarrow F^d \left\{\begin{matrix}=\\\geq\end{matrix}\right\} 0 \qquad \text{for } t \geq t_o,$$

$$(III.106a)\quad \hat{P}_H = 0 \qquad \text{for } t_o \leq t < t^*,$$

and

$$(III.106b)\quad \hat{P}_H = -\frac{m}{P_H} + r + \alpha\delta \qquad \text{for } t \geq t^*.$$

As is known from the previous comments, the tax-induced change in the tax payer's portfolio causes an increase in the price of vacant land in the planning period. As can be read from conditions (III.104) and (III.105), the landlord reacts to this increase in investment costs with a rise in the capital intensity of new housing units as well as with a reduction of his initial construction plans. This decline in the propensity to invest is reflected in the leftward shift of the supply-curve illustrated in the left quadrant of figure 12. In chapter II the fact that the numerical value of the differential dH/dB varies directly with the horizontal distance of the supply curve from the vertical axis is derived from relation

$$\text{(II.55)'} \quad P_H = 1/\varphi'[\varphi^{-1}(|dH/dB|)], \quad dP_H/d(|dH/dB|) > 0.$$

Figure 12

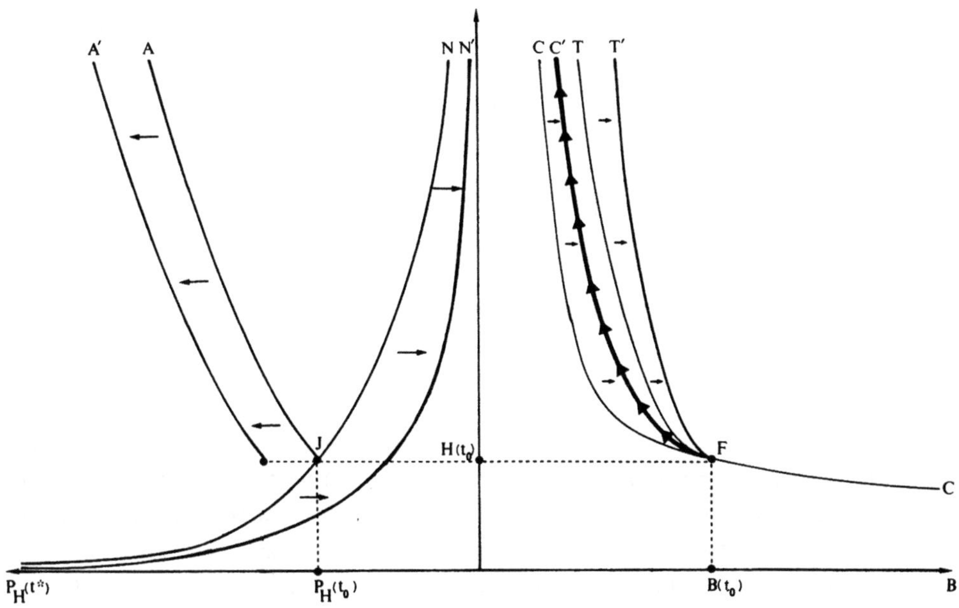

In addition to the tax-induced increase in investment costs the landlord also experiences a tax-induced reduction in the rentability of the housing stock existing in the planning period. This economically intuitive statement - because of the preferential tax treatment of income earned by vacant land housing stock is the less desirable asset - can be proved by referring to equilibrium conditions (III.101b), (III.104) and (III.105). From the latter two conditions the growth equations $\hat{P}_H = \beta\hat{\varepsilon}$ and $\hat{\varepsilon} = \hat{P}_B$ can be derived easily.

Using the modified Hotelling-rule stated in condition (III.101b), the equilibrium growth rate of the house price therefore is

$$\text{(III.107)} \quad \hat{P}_H = \beta(1 - \tau_I)r.$$

According to (III.107) capital gains incurred in the housing stock shrink in response to the tax exemption of capital gains accrued in the stock of vacant land. Consequently the user cost of capital in the housing sector must be higher compared to a situation where a comprehensive income tax is levied. Solving condition (III.106b) for P_H and using the relationship found in (III.107) results in the function for the demand curve N' in the left quadrant of figure 12:

$$\text{(III.108)} \quad P_H = \frac{m(\frac{a}{H})}{(1-\tau_I)r(1-\beta) + \alpha\delta}.$$

Comparing function (III.108) with the corresponding laissez-faire relationship, it is easy to see that the value of the ratio on the right-hand side of equation (III.108) decreases under the influence of the tax regulations discussed in this section. For this reason the graph of (III.108) must lie to the right of the laissez-faire demand curve N.

Referring to figure 12 the dynamic effects of the tax exemption of capital gains accrued in the stock of vacant land can be deducted in a straightforward way. The landlord is not willing to defray the increase in the cost of building land in the initial period t_o. Instead of this he temporarily suspends the construction of new housing units. Construction activities will be resumed when as a consequence of the steady increase in the demand for housing services the value of the marginal product of land again equals the desired price of land. Despite this transitory halt in housing investment, the stock of housing units will exceed and the rental rate will fall short of their laissez-faire level in finite time. The landlord anticipates the landowner's willingness to increase the supply of vacant land in the long run, compared to the tax-free situation. The associated decrease in construction costs will cause an acceleration in the landlord's future propensity to invest. Substituting condition (III.101b) into the general growth equation (II.71) for the housing stock yields

$$\text{(III.109)} \quad \hat{H} = \hat{a} - \eta\beta(1 - \tau_I)r;$$

Equation (III.109) provides the formal confirmation that after the exemption of capital gains accrued in the stock of vacant land from the comprehensive income tax base, the growth in the stock of housing units accelerates. Since (III.109) also allows for conclusions concerning the dynamics of the supply of housing services, it follows that given the time path of demand for these services the house rent grows at a lower than Pareto-optimal rate.

It is also important to note that from an efficiency point of view the stock of vacant land in every point of time beyond t_o is bigger than desirable. The formal proof of this statement can be derived by substituting equilibrium condition (III.101b) into the general equation (II.76), the latter defining the shrinkage rate of stock B.

b) Taxing Capital Gains on Realization

That the tax exemption of capital gains accrued in vacant land encourages the holding of vacant land is a fact tax authorities and politicians should be worried about. But especially in the political field proposals suggesting the taxation of capital gains have been repeatedly blocked in the past:

- The usual argument promoted against taxing accrued capital gains is that it is unfeasible because of administrative difficulties;

- the proposal of taxing capital gains on realization is declined with the very popular argument that it induces the landowner to postpone the sale of vacant land. The intuition behind this argument is that the deferral of land sales gives the landowner the chance to defer his tax payments, thus leading to a reduction of the tax burden (measured in present values).

The analytical framework of our analysis is certainly not appropriate to settle disagreements concerning the first argument. But it should be noted that the recent tax literature boasts a number of proposals on how to implement a tax on accrued capital gains in an administratively manageable way.

However, the second argument exhibits a noticable lack of logical consistency. In arguing against the taxation of realized capital gains it makes no sense to refer to the tax-free situation. A proviso against this form of taxation can be justified only by the proof that a tax on realized capital gains <u>amplifies</u> the incentive to postpone the development of vacant land induced by current tax regulations. The following analysis will show that the opposite holds.

If capital gains are taxed upon realization, tax revenues are independent of changes in the market value of the stock B. It is the change in the market value of the flow of vacant land, F^s, consumed in a given period that is subject to taxation. This change of value is equivalent to the difference between the going resource price, P_B, and the resource price that prevailed in a certain base period. Let t_o be this base period. Revenues of a tax on realized capital gains in a given period t are equal to

$$\text{(III.110)} \quad T_I^{LO}(t) = \tau_I[P_B(t)-P_B(t_o)]F^s(t).$$

Using equation (III.110) the landowner's planning problem reads

$$\text{(III.111)} \quad \max_{\{F^s\}} M(t_o) \equiv \int_{t_o}^{\infty} [P_B(t)F^s(t)-T_I^{LO}(t)]\exp[-z(1-\tau_I)r(t-t^*)]dt,$$

under the constraints (II.1), (II.17a) and (II.45).

The Hamiltonian corresponding to (III.111) is

$$(\text{III.112})\quad \mathcal{H} = (1 - \tau_I)P_B F^s + z\tau_I P_B(t_o)F^s - \lambda_B F^s .$$

In equation (III.112) the parameter λ_B represents the shadow value of the stock of vacant land. Differentiating (III.112) with respect to the variables F^s and B and considering the canonical equation for B the following necessary conditions for the optimal path of land supply can be obtained:

$$(\text{III.113})\quad \lambda_B = (1 - z\tau_I)P_B + z\tau_I P_B(t_o),$$

$$(\text{III.114})\quad \dot{\lambda}_B - z(1 - \tau_I)r\lambda_B = 0.$$

Because $P_B(t_o)$ is constant, it follows from (III.113) that

$$\dot{\lambda}_B = (1 - z\tau_I)\dot{P}_B.$$

Subsituting this relationship into (III.114) we obtain

$$(\text{III.115a})\quad \hat{P}_B = 0 \qquad \text{for } t_o \leq t < t^*,$$

$$(\text{III.115b})\quad \hat{P}_B(t) = (1 - \tau_I)r + \tau_I r \frac{P_B(t_o)}{P_B(t)} \qquad \text{for } t > t^*.$$

Equation (III.115b) states that in every point of time after the imposition of an income tax including the taxation of realized capital gains the land price grows at a higher rate compared to the situation where the taxation of capital gains is entirely foregone [only for $t=\infty$ both growth rates are the same because of $\lim_{t\to\infty} P_B(t)=\infty$]. This result gives rise to the surprising conclusion that there is <u>no</u> "lock-in" effect induced by the taxation of realized capital gains. On the contrary, including realized capital gains in the income tax base <u>reduces</u> the incentive to postpone the development of vacant land.

The economic intuition behind this result is straightforward. Suppose that in addition to a tax on interest income there is a sales tax instead of a capital gains tax imposed; tax base is the value $P_B F^S$ of land transactions in a given period. Because the price P_B and therefore the tax base grows at a rate which is equal to the discount rate $(1 - \tau_I)r$, the imposition of such a tax obviously would have no impact on the resource owner's sale plans. The difference between a tax on realized capital gains and the above sales tax is that a tax on realized capital gains is assessed only on the appreciation in the resource price between the base period t_o and the date of sale, leaving the initial price $P_B(t_o)$ tax-free. Therefore a tax on realized capital gains is equivalent to a combination of a (neutral) sales tax and a government subsidy on the sale of the resource, worth $\tau_I P_B(t_o)$ for every unit sold. Obviously, the <u>current value</u> of this subsidy is independent of the date on which the transaction takes place. Therefore, the <u>present value</u> of this subsidy is greater the earlier a given quantity of vacant land is sold. Condition (III.115b) also states that the tax induced incentive to advance the sale of a given quantity F^S is greater the earlier the sale of the same quantity would have been planned in a tax-free economy. For $t \to \infty$ this incentive approaches zero because the relative importance of the tax subsidy, compared to the tax liability, approaches zero.

Equation (III.115b) also states that in comparison to the tax-free situation or to a situation where a comprehensive income tax is imposed, the assessment of an income tax including realized rather than accrued capital gains unambiguously results in a deferment of land sales. This can be seen from rearranging condition (III.115b) to

$$\text{(III.115b)'} \quad \hat{P}_B(t) = r - \frac{\tau_I r[P_B(t) - P_B(t_o)]}{P_B(t)} \qquad \text{for } t \geqq t^*.$$

The tax-induced decrease in the land price's growth rate indicates that the landowner responds to the imposition of an income tax of the type discussed above with an adjustment of his portfolio in favour of vacant land. A glance on the transversality condition for stock B confirms that as a consequence of this reaction the supply of vacant land beyond t_o has to be higher than it would have been in the laissez-faire economy. Given the time path of land demand, this change in sale plans causes the reduction of the growth rate described in (III.115b). But is has to be stressed that it is not the taxation of realized capital gains which is responsible for this reaction. The postponement rather is the result of the collision of two opposite effects:

- First, as shown in case a) of this section the exemption of accrued capital gains from the tax base provides an incentive to postpone the sale of the resource. In equation (III.115b) the term $(1 - \tau_I)r$ illustrates this incentive algebraically;
- Second, the inclusion of realized capital gains in the tax base provides an incentive to advance the sale of vacant land, this incentive is represented by the term $r\tau_I P_B(t_o)/P_B(t)$ in equation (III.115b).

On balance, the above tax regulations result in a postponement of sales. But this arises because of the exclusion of accrued capital gains from the tax base rather than from a taxation of realized capital gains per se.

3.2.2 Income taxation of the landlord

Current income tax regulations fail to fulfill the requirements for an uniform taxation of housing income. One reason for this failure is that a prospective houseowner who decides to build his home by himself instead of buying it is treated preferentially, compared to the prospective owner-buyer. Because the value added by laying bricks, painting window frames, etc., although always representing income from an economic point of view, is tax free as long as these services are not traded in markets, the prospective owner might (legally) reduce the cost of his housing investment by carrying out such activities himself. The incentive to do this lasts as long as the opportunity cost of do-it-yourself activities - loss in wage income net of tax and/or in utility-bearing leisure - fall short of their benefits.

In the partial equilibrium context of this analysis the associated inefficiencies are easy to localize - the discriminating income tax treatment of home buyers violates the condition for an optimal intersectoral allocation of construction services. Corresponding welfare losses can be illustrated by the plane of a Harberger triangle. Moreover, additional welfare losses might be induced if the owner-builder is not experienced in do-it-yourself activities, thus causing a reduction of welfare gains from specialization.

However, in a general equilibrium framework these welfare losses are at least partially offset by the welfare gain that results from a distortion of the individual work-leisure choice. Compared to a situation where the monetary equivalents of non-traded services are subject to taxation, the exemption of such services induces the individual tax-payer to change his work-leisure-choice in favor of work, thus coming closer to his Pareto-optimal labor supply.

In what follows we will restrain from considering tax induced inefficiences within the acquisition stage of housing units and focus on inefficiencies arising during the utilization period of these units.

There are two reasons for possible welfare-losses incurred in the taxation of housing income. First, housing income is taxed differently, depending on whether this income results from renting or from owner-occupation. Second, in both cases the definition of the respective income tax base deviates significantly from the ideal defined in equation (III.68).

a) Taxing Rental Income

If the landlord rents his stock of housing units, his taxable income is the figure obtained after a number of deductions have been subtracted from total rental revenues, m H. In accordance with equation (III.68) current income tax laws declare mortgage interest payments as tax deductible. But that is about the sole correspondence to the base of a (neutral) comprehensive income tax.

Instead of including changes in the market value of the existing housing stock, $\dot{P}_H H - P_H \alpha\delta H$, into the tax base, today's regulations provide for an allowance based on the purchase value of construction services embodied in that stock. In terms of our analysis, the dynamic behaviour of the stock of construction services, K, can be described by the motion equation

$$(III.28) \quad \dot{K} = F^d \varepsilon - (\delta K - E).$$

At any given point of time the change in the stock of construction services is the net result of new construction, maintenance, and deterioration. Equation (III.28) implies that the revenue authorities apply the "true" rate of deterioration, δ. But catchwords like "accelerated depreciation" indicate that this is not the case. Usually for tax purposes a depreciation rate, μ, is assigned that exceeds the rate δ.

Moreover, maintenance investment does not enter the asset side as far as income taxation is concerned - expenses for maintenance are immediately and completely deductible from the income tax base. This implies that the parameter E is excluded from the base for depreciation allowances.

Taking these deviations into account, the measure of construction services for income-tax purposes, K^*, changes its value over time according to the following equation:

$$(III.116) \quad \dot{K}^* = F^d \varepsilon - \mu K^*.$$

The term μK^* represents the value of the landlord's depreciation allowances in a given period.

Consequently, the landlord's income tax liabilities are defined as

$$(III.117) \quad T_I^{LL} = \tau_I (mH - E - rD - \mu K^*),$$

the parameter τ_I again representing the (proportional) income tax rate. With respect to (III.117) the distribution net of tax, A, in a given period adopts the value

$$(III.118) \quad A = z(1-\tau_I)(mH - E - rD) + S - F^d \varepsilon - P_B F^d + z\tau_I \mu K^*.$$

Therefore, the landlord's planning problem reads

$$(\text{III.119}) \quad \max_{\{S,E,\varepsilon,F^d\}} M_H \equiv \int_{t_0}^{\infty} A(t) \exp\,[-z(1-\tau_I)r(t-t^*)]\,dt,$$

under the constraints (II.2), (II.3), (II.9), (II.10), (II.14), (II.16), (II.17a), (III.116), and (III.118).

The Hamiltonian corresponding to this planning problem is

$$(\text{III.120}) \quad \mathcal{H} = z(1-\tau_I)(mH-E-rD) + S - F^d\varepsilon - P_B F^d + z\tau_I \mu K^*$$
$$+ P_H[F^d\varphi(\varepsilon) - z(\alpha\delta H-E)]$$
$$+ \lambda_{K^*}(F^d\varepsilon - z\mu K^*)$$
$$- \lambda_D S.$$

The parameter λ_{K^*} is the shadow value of stock K^*.

That the current tax treatment of housing income has no impact on the landlord's financing behaviour can be proven by differentiating (III.12) with respect to S. Because of

$$\lambda_D \equiv \frac{\partial M_H}{\partial D} = -1,$$

the partial derivative $\partial\mathcal{H}/\partial S$ implies

$$(\text{III.121}) \quad 1 + \lambda_D = 0 \Rightarrow EF \sim CF.$$

Since interest payments are tax deductible and interest income is subject to taxation, the costs of credit financing and the (opportunity) costs of equity financing are the same. For this reason the landlord could not derive any advantage from altering the financing structure of his housing stock.

From the above it follows that the second term on the right-hand side of optimality conditions

(II.24) $$\frac{\partial \mathcal{H}}{\partial E} = \frac{\partial \mathcal{H}}{\partial E} + \frac{\partial \mathcal{H}}{\partial S} \cdot \frac{\partial S}{\partial E},$$

(II.28) $$\frac{\partial \mathcal{H}}{\partial \varepsilon} = \frac{\partial \mathcal{H}}{\partial \varepsilon} + \frac{\partial \mathcal{H}}{\partial S} \cdot \frac{\partial S}{\partial \varepsilon},$$

(II.29) $$\frac{\partial \mathcal{H}}{\partial F^d} = \frac{\partial \mathcal{H}}{\partial F^d} + \frac{\partial \mathcal{H}}{\partial S} \cdot \frac{\partial S}{\partial F^d},$$

(II.30) $$-\frac{\partial \mathcal{H}}{\partial H} = -\left[\frac{\partial \mathcal{H}}{\partial H} + \frac{\partial \mathcal{H}}{\partial S} \cdot \frac{\partial S}{\partial H}\right]$$

vanishes(it is $\partial \mathcal{H}/\partial S = 0$).

Given the assumption about the house price made in chapter II ($P_H > 1$ for all $t \geq t_o$) the time path of maintenance investment also remains unaffected by the deviations from the comprehensive income tax described above. However, the effective cost of maintenance decrease owing to taxation.

Differentiating (III.120) with respect to E, we achieve

(III.122) $$P_H > 1 - z\tau_I.$$

It was shown in section III.1 of this analysis that an efficient taxation of housing income implies that maintenance expenses must not appear in the income tax base. Allowing the immediate deduction of maintenance, the public sector shares in maintenance cost according to the imposed income tax rate.

While the landlord maintains his initial financing and renovation plans, his plans concerning the construction of new rental accomodation vary considerably from those prevailing in a tax free economy. To see this, the Hamiltonian in (III.20) must be differentiated with respect to the variables F^d, ε, H, and K^*.

The necessary conditions for a solution to these planning problems imply

$$\text{(III.123)} \quad P_H \varphi'(\varepsilon) = 1-\lambda_{K^*} \qquad \text{for } t \geq t^*,$$

$$\text{(III.124)} \quad \frac{\beta}{\alpha}\varepsilon\,(1-\lambda_{K^*}) \left\{\begin{smallmatrix} < \\ = \end{smallmatrix}\right\} P_B \Rightarrow \dot{F}^d \left\{\begin{smallmatrix} = \\ \geq \end{smallmatrix}\right\} 0 \qquad \text{for } t \geq t_o,$$

$$\text{(III.125a)} \quad \hat{P}_H = 0 \qquad \text{for } t_o \leq t < t^*,$$

$$\text{(III.125b)} \quad \hat{P}_H = -\frac{(1-\tau_I)m}{P_H} + (1-\tau_I)r + \alpha\delta \qquad \text{for } t \geq t^*,$$

$$\text{(III.126)} \quad \lambda_{K^*} = \frac{\tau_I \mu}{(1-\tau_I)r+\mu} .$$

The right-hand side of condition (III.123) states that the per-unit cost of construction services - one dollar per unit in the tax-free situation - decreases due to actual income tax regulations. Equation (III.126) describes the shadow value λ_{K*} as the present value of income tax refunds allowed by the marginal service unit. In fact it turns out that current "depreciation allowances" are actually a governmental subsidy on the use of construction services (because actual income tax laws only allow for the deduction of historic acquisition costs, this subsidy decreases in value in the presence of inflation). Knowing this, it is not surprising at all that in response to the imposition of the tax the landlord alters the combination of inputs, reducing the input of land; as stated in condition (III.124) the capital intensity of land varies directly with the shadow value λ_{K*}, all other things equal. Moreover, the tax subsidy on construction services leads to a reduction in the production cost of new rental accomodation, thus making investment in rental accomodation more attractive. This follows from conditions (III.123) and (III.124), considering the assumed properties of the construction technology, i.e. $\varphi' > 0$, $\varphi'' < 0$. Both conditions can be fulfilled simultaneously only if the house price, P_H, prevailing after the imposition of the tax falls short of its laissez-faire counterpart. Given the demand for housing services, this implies that the optimal housing stock in the after-tax equilibrium exceeds its laissez-faire level.

Despite the discriminatory income tax treatment of building land, the laissez-faire relationships between the endogenous growth rates remain unchanged. From (III.123) it follows that

$$\text{(III.127)} \quad \hat{P}_H = \beta\hat{\varepsilon},$$

and (III.124) implies

$$\text{(III.128)} \quad \hat{\varepsilon} = \hat{P}_B.$$

A glance at condition (III.125b) confirms that present income tax regulations also influence the user cost of wealth in the housing sector; however, confined to the partial equilibrium framework of our analysis, it is not possible to say whether these costs decrease or increase. Choosing the Pareto-optimal portfolio as a reference point, equation (III.125b) shows that the user cost

- increases because the deterioration-induced loss in housing property does not enter the income tax base;
- decreases, because capital gains accrued in the housing stock are not subject to taxation.

Whether present income tax laws prefer or discriminate against the housing stock relative to other assets obviously depends upon the change of the market value $P_H H$ over time. Provided that income earned by alternative assets is entirely subject to taxation, for $\dot{P}_H H - P_H \alpha\delta H > 0$ (< 0) the above deviations from a comprehensive income tax base tend to encourage (discourage) investment in rental accomodation.

It is important to note that these results only hold if we examine the landlord's planning problem in isolation. The description of tax effects will be different if the landowner's reactions to the tax exemption of capital gains are taken into account. Because capital gains accrued in the stock of vacant land are also tax exempt, an investment in housing stock so far yields no specific advantages. However, there remains the disadvantage of deterioration-induced capital losses not being deductible from the income tax base. Given this disadvantage housing stock is unambigeously the less desirable asset. The formal proof for this intuitive result can be found by noting that according to the after-tax equilibrium growth rates in (III.108b), (III.127) and (III.128), the landlord responds to the landowner's tax-induced alteration of sale plans in a way that causes the house price to grow at a lower rate than the laissez-faire rate:

$$\text{(III.129)} \quad \hat{P}_H = \beta \hat{P}_B = \beta(1 - \tau_I)r.$$

Substituting (III.129) into condition (III.125b) yields, after rearranging terms, the function of the demand curve N' in figure 13.

$$\text{(III.130)} \quad P_H = \frac{m(\frac{a}{H})}{(1-\beta)r + \frac{\alpha\delta}{1-\tau_I}} .$$

Comparing the demand function in (III.130) with the corresponding laissez-faire relationship (that can be derived from (III.130) by setting $\tau_I = 0$), one recognizes that c.p. the house price decreases in response to income taxation, indicating a relative decrease in the profitability of the housing stock as an asset. In our graphical analysis the consequences of the resulting tax induced portfolio adjustment can be illustrated by a shift of the demand curve to the right. This is done in figure 13, where N represents the laissez-faire demand curve.

Figure 13 also exhibits a rightward shift of the supply curve. There are two causes which are responsible for this shift. The first is the reaction of landlord and landowner to the tax exemption of capital gains accrued in the stock of vacant land. These reactions also cause the shift of the curves shown in the right quadrant of figure 13. The previous section contains the detailed explanation of the economic intuition behind the graphical presentation. Second, as pointed out above, depreciation allowances not only favour the use of construction services in the production of housing units but also cause a reduction in the overall production costs. That this results in an immediate increase in the landlord's propensity to invest can be proven by substituting the inverse of optimality condition (III.123) into the general supply-

Figure 13

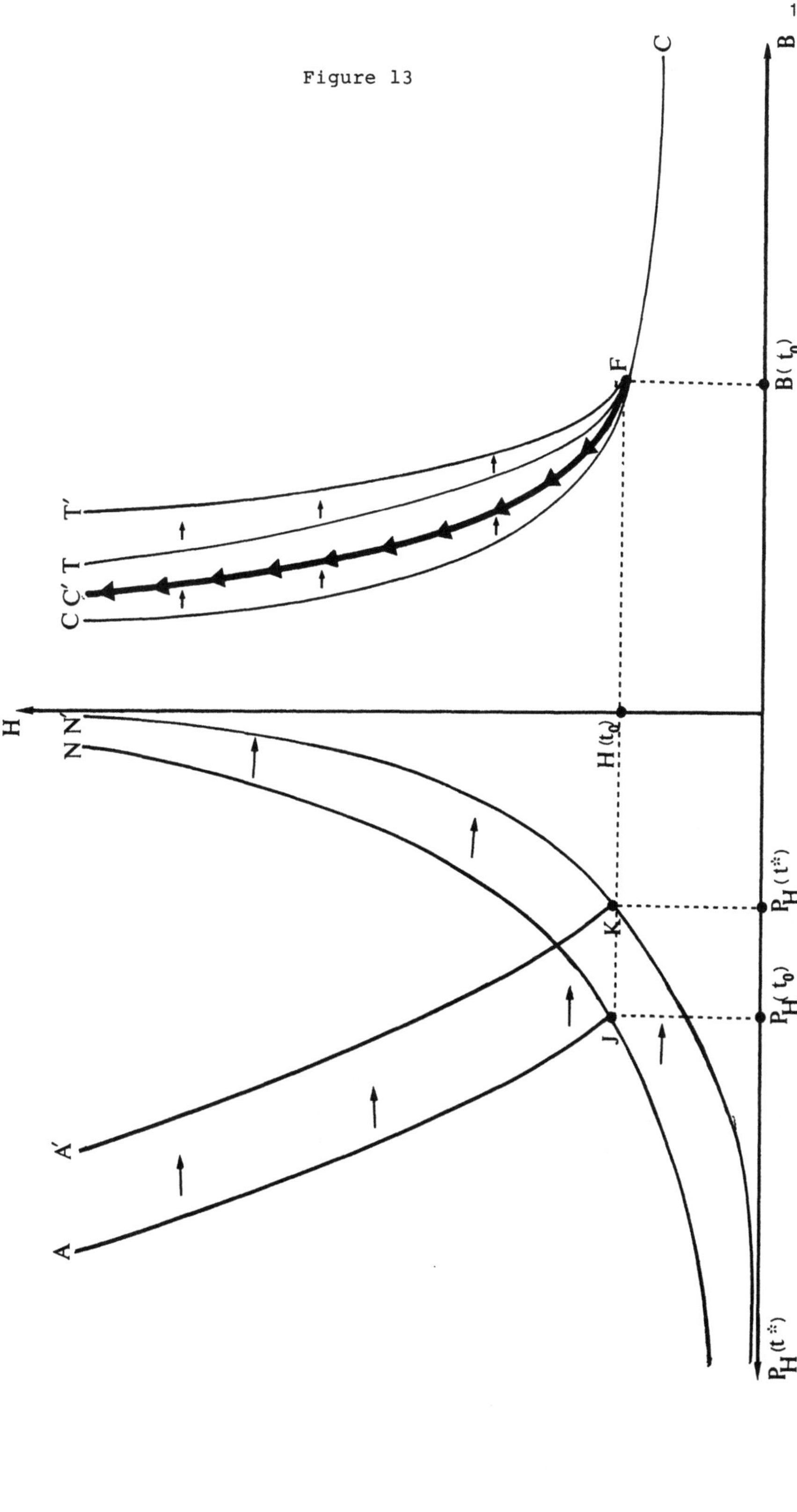

function (II.79). This operation generates

$$(III.131) \quad H(t^*) = \Phi\{\varphi[\varphi'^{-1}(\frac{K^{*\,1-\lambda}}{P_H(t^*)})]\}.$$

Considering that Φ', φ', $-\varphi'' < 0$, it follows from (III.131) that for any level of the house price $P_H(t^*)$, the corresponding optimal housing stock $H(t^*)$ is bigger than in a world with a comprehensive income tax.

Since both, the demand curve and the supply curve simultaneously shift to the right, the short-run incidence of the income tax regulations discussed so far is ambigeous. A clear cut statement can be made only if detailed information is available about the relative size of the two tax-induced counteracting effects.
Figure 13 features the special case where the advantage of the tax subsidy on construction services just offsets the disadvantage of not being allowed to deduct capital losses caused by deterioration. In this special case the tax on income from real estate property is neutral as far as the short run is concerned. Also conceivable are scenarios in which one effect dominates the other, leading to either a short-term construction boom or a temporary halt in construction activities.

Since the tax on rental income does not affect the economy's growth characteristics, any distortion occuring in the short run will persist in any future period. If the imposition of an income tax akin to current tax laws induces a short-term construction boom, then in every period beyond t_o the housing stock will exceed its laissez-faire level. Also the rental rate, the house price, the supply of vacant land, and the stock of vacant land will fall short of their respective laissez-faire levels. The opposite holds if the landlord's initial reaction consists in a transitory investment stop.

Whatever the reactions of the rental market in the short run, it will always pay for the landlord to choose a higher capital intensity of land because of the preferential treatment of construction services.

We can summarize the results derived in this chapter as follows: although catchwords like accelerated depreciation suggest an unambigeously preferential treatment of housing property by current income tax regulations it is impossible to say whether the housing sector compared to the laissez-faire allocation benefits or suffers from the deviations from a comprehensive income tax typical for income tax laws in force in almost all Western economies.

b) Taxing Income from Owner-Occupation

Owner-occupation differs from renting in one economically significant aspect: in the case of owner-occupation the consumption good "housing service" is not traded in a market; therefore there are no monetary flows related to the exchange of this good. However, the absence of a direct monetary measure does not necessarily imply that housing income cannot be determined if the landlord decides to live in his own house. The vast literature on imputed rent confirms that. One way to estimate income from owner-occupation is to assume the gross revenues earned by comparable, but rented housing units as imputed rent, add the change in market value, $\dot{P}_H H - P_H \alpha\delta H$, and allow for the deduction of all interest liabilities related to housing property. The resulting tax base thus will come close to the ideal defined in (III.68).

An alternative measure for the income earned by owner-occupation is the product between the market interest rate, r, and the market value of equity tied into the housing stock, $P_H H - D$. A simple arbitrage consideration shows why an income tax assessed on the flow $r(P_H H - D)$ has to be neutral. At the beginning of every period the owner-occupier can choose between two alternatives. The first is to sell the stock of housing units at the actual market value, $P_H H$. After paying off his debt, he can invest the remaining amount, $P_H H - D$, in financial assets, guaranteeing him an annual gross income stream of $r(P_H H - D)$ dollars. The second alternative is to keep his stock of housing units; the income stream resulting from this alternative is $mH + \dot{P}_H H - rD - P_H \alpha\delta H$. An arbitrage equilibrium obviously requires the owner-occupier's indifference between both options. Proceeding on the assumption of rationality, this indifference implies that both flows, $[r(P_H H - D)]$ and $[mH + \dot{P}_H H - rD - P_H \alpha\delta H]$, have the same value. Correspondingly it will make no difference to the landlord whether he has to pay taxes of $\tau_I r(P_H H-D)$ or $\tau_I(mH-\dot{P}_H H-rD-P_H\alpha\delta H)$ dollars.

Despite the possibility of taxing imputed rental income, in practise the owner-occupier can enjoy the benefits of his housing property unburdened from taxation. This holds by and large for European as well as North American countries. However, there is one peculiar characteristic in the U.S.-income tax law that makes the income tax treatment of U.S.-owner-occupiers unique: despite the fact that the imputed rent is tax exempt, interest payments related to owner-occupied housing property are tax deductible. In the following equation the parameter γ_2 indicates this specific regulation:

$$\text{(III.132)} \quad T_I^{LL} = -\gamma_2\tau_I rD.$$

Equation (III.132) contains the formal description of the owner-occupier's tax "liabilities". The parameter γ_2 can adopt the values "0" and "1", the value "1" indicating the situation in the U.S.

Using the information provided by equation (III.132), the distribution in a given period is

$$\text{(III.133)} \quad A = z(mH-E-rD) - F^d\varepsilon - P_B F^d + z\gamma_2\tau_I rD + S.$$

Since the market value of the owner-occupied housing stock is the sum of present values of actual and future distributions, the owner-occupiers planning problem reads

$$\text{(III.134)} \quad \max_{\{S,E,F^d,\varepsilon\}} M_H(t_o) \equiv \int_{t_o}^{\infty} A(t)\exp[-z(1-\tau_I)r(t-t^*)]dt$$

under the constraints (II.2), (II.3), (II.9), (II.10), (II.14), (II.16), (II.17a) and (III.133). The Hamiltonian for this control problem is

$$(III.135)\quad \mathcal{K} = z(mH-E-rD) - F^d\varepsilon - P_B F^d + z\gamma_2\tau_I rD + S.$$

$$+ P_H[F^d\varphi(\varepsilon) - z(\alpha\delta H - E)]$$

$$+ \lambda_D S .$$

To determine the owner-occupier's financing preferences, we have to differentiate (III.135) with respect to S.

$$(III.136)\quad \frac{\partial\mathcal{K}}{\partial S} = 1 + \lambda_D \left\{\begin{matrix}<\\=\\>\end{matrix}\right\} 0 \Rightarrow EF \left\{\begin{matrix}>\\\sim\\<\end{matrix}\right\} CF .$$

From the definition of the shadow value of the stock D it follows that

$$(III.137)\quad \lambda_D = - \frac{(1-\gamma_2\tau_I)r}{(1-\tau_I)r} .$$

The numerical value of parameter λ_D obviously depends upon the value of parameter γ_2. In the case where interest payments are tax deductible ($\gamma_2 = 1$) it is $\lambda_D = -1$. Substituting this into (III.136) yields

$$(III.138)\quad EF \sim CF \qquad \text{for } \gamma_2 = 1.$$

The U.S. income tax regulations thus ensure that the owner-occupier does not develop a preference for one of the two financing alternatives open to him. The effective cost of every dollar borrowed are equal to the opportunity cost of every dollar equity tied into his housing stock. Therefore no gain can be achieved from changing the financing structure of stock H in favor of either alternative.

In the case where interest payments are not tax deductible, the landlord will reveal an unambigeous preference for equity financing. This is because the opportunity cost of this alternative, i.e. $(1-\tau_I)r$ dollar interest forgone for every dollar equity, now are lower than the cost of borrowing. The preference can be derived formally by setting $\gamma_2 = 0$, what in turn implies $\lambda_D < -1$ or

$$\text{(III.139)} \quad EF > CF \qquad \text{for } \gamma_2 = 0.$$

Although credit financing does not qualify as a rational option, a "poor" owner-occupier who does not dispose of enough equity is forced to choose this alternative. It is plaubsible to suspect that this tax-induced incompatibility between preferences and possibilities also influences the "poor" owner-occupiers investment behavior.

To detect the impact of the respective financing decision on the propensity to invest, one has to refer to the general conditions

$$\text{(II.24)} \quad \frac{\partial \mathcal{K}}{\partial E} = \frac{\partial \mathcal{K}}{\partial E} + \frac{\partial \mathcal{K}}{\partial S} \cdot \frac{\partial S}{\partial E},$$

$$\text{(II.28)} \quad \frac{\partial \mathcal{K}}{\partial \varepsilon} = \frac{\partial \mathcal{K}}{\partial \varepsilon} + \frac{\partial \mathcal{K}}{\partial S} \cdot \frac{\partial S}{\partial \varepsilon},$$

$$\text{(II.29)} \quad \frac{\partial \mathcal{K}}{\partial F^d} = \frac{\partial \mathcal{K}}{\partial F^d} + \frac{\partial \mathcal{K}}{\partial S} \cdot \frac{\partial S}{\partial F^d},$$

$$\text{(II.30)} \quad -\frac{\partial \mathcal{K}}{\partial H} = -\left[\frac{\partial \mathcal{K}}{\partial H} + \frac{\partial \mathcal{K}}{\partial S} \cdot \frac{\partial \mathcal{K}}{\partial H}\right].$$

As is shown above the deductibility of interest payments from the income tax base implies $\partial \mathcal{K}/\partial S = 0$. In the case where interest payments are not tax deductible, the partial derivative $\partial \mathcal{K}/\partial S$ is smaller than zero, an indication that equity financing is preferred. Given that the owner-occupier is "wealthy", i.e. capable to finance his housing investment with his own money, it is

$$\text{(III.14)} \quad \frac{\partial S}{\partial E} = \frac{\partial S}{\partial \varepsilon} = \frac{\partial S}{\partial F^d} = \frac{\partial S}{\partial H} = 0.$$

Therefore, in both cases the second term on the right-hand side of conditions (II.24), (II.28)-(II.30) vanishes. Consequently the necessary conditions for the owner-occupiers maintenance and investment plans read

$$\text{(III.141)}\quad E = \begin{cases} 0 & \text{for } t_o \leq t < t^*, \\ \alpha\delta H & \text{for } t \geq t^*, \end{cases}$$

$$\text{(III.142)}\quad P_H \varphi'(\varepsilon) = 1 \qquad \text{for } t \geq t_o,$$

$$\text{(III.143)}\quad \frac{\beta}{\alpha}\varepsilon \begin{Bmatrix} < \\ = \end{Bmatrix} P_B \Rightarrow F^d \begin{Bmatrix} = \\ \geq \end{Bmatrix} 0 \qquad \text{for } t \geq t_o,$$

$$\text{(III.144a)}\quad \hat{P}_H = 0 \qquad \text{for } t_o \leq t < t^*,$$

$$\text{(III.144b)}\quad \hat{P}_H = - \frac{m}{P_H} + (1-\tau_I)\, r + \alpha\delta \qquad \text{for } t \geq t^*.$$

Condition (III.141) states that the landlord sticks to his laissez-faire maintenance plan or the plan chosen under the regime of a comprehensive income tax, respectively. Since the cost of financing and the treatment of maintenance expenditures within the two alternatives discussed above are the same as in the case where housing income is taxed efficiently, this result is not surprising. Also the initial decision concerning the choice of the optimal capital intensity remains unchanged, indicating that contrary to the taxation of rental income the tax regulations discussed above do not discriminate against the use of land in producing housing units. Conditions (III.142) and (III.143) confirm this statement formally.

Nevertheless, the tax exemption of his imputed rental income affects the owner-occupier's housing investment plans. This can be read from condition (III.144b). Provided either that interest payments are tax deductible or that the owner-occupier is capable of equity financing, the present tax treatment of owner-occupation leads to a decrease in the user cost of capital in this sector. The net rate of return on every dollar invested in housing stock, $[m/P_H + \hat{P}_H - \alpha\delta]$, now has to cover the lower opportunity cost of the same dollar compared to the case of a comprehensive income tax, i.e. interest forgegone <u>net</u> of tax $(1-\tau_I)r$. The decrease in user cost indicates an increase in the profitability of owner-occupied housing investment. The resulting rise in the propensity to invest can be explained easily by considering that the tax exemption of imputed rental income provides a (legal) loop hole for tax avoidance.

The consequences of the preferential income tax treatment of the interest bearing asset "owner-occupied house" can be illustrated graphically by a leftward shift of the laissez-faire demand curve in figure 6. Solving condition (III.144b) for P_H and considering the impact of the tax exemption of capital gains accrued in the stock of vacant land (being reflected in (III.129)) yields the functional relationship for the after-tax demand curve N' in figure 14:

$$\text{(III.145)} \quad P_H = \frac{m[\frac{a}{H}]}{[(1-\tau_I)(1-\beta)r + \alpha\delta]}.$$

The comparison with the respective laissez-faire relationship shows that the value of the fraction in condition (III.145) varies directly with the value of the tax rate. For every rental rate m and thus, since the demand for housing services is given, for any given level of the stock H the house price exceeds its corresponding laissez-faire level.

Figure 14

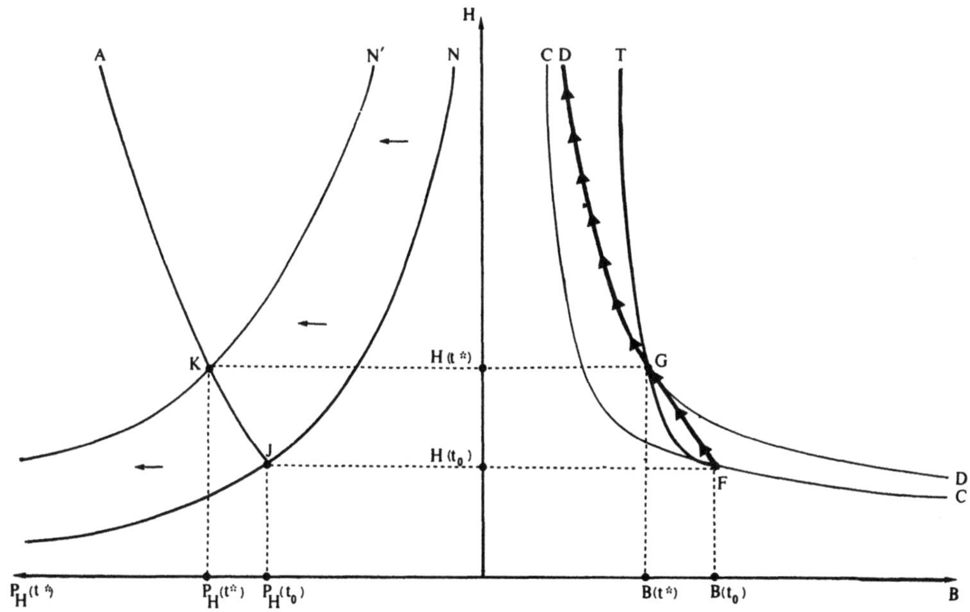

Figure 14 shows that the present tax treatment of imputed rental income stimulates construction activities in the short run. Starting from the equilibrium situation indicated by J and F, respectively, the introduction of an income tax that leaves imputed rental income tax-free causes a temporary construction boom for new buildings. As a result of this process the stock of housing units adjusts from its initial level $H(t_o)$ to the new optimal level $H(t^*)$. After the end of the meta-time period the system evolves along the path FD . Since the tax treatment of imputed rental income has no impact on the endogenous growth rates*), at every point of time beyond t^*

- the stock of housing units is larger, and
- the stock of vacant land is smaller

than they would have been in the tax-free situation. Also the time path for

- the capital intensity of land and
- the price of vacant land (in order to induce the landowner to support his additional investment plans, the landlord has to pay a higher price for land)

will be located above their laissez-faire levels. On the other hand the level of rental rates and thus the level of house prices will stay permanently below the respective laissez-faire paths: only if the landlord is willing to accept a lower rental rate the households are willing to purchase the increased supply of housing services.

All these results are derived under the assumption that interest liabilities are income tax deductible or that the landlord disposes of sufficient equity to finance housing investment in the cheapest way.

If instead interest liabilities are not tax deductible and the landlord is a "poor" investor, who cannot opt for the relatively cheap financing alternative, the impacts of current income tax regulations are different. As described in chapter II, the landlord's credibility in a given period is restricted to the increase in the market value of stock H in this period:

$$\text{(III.146)} \quad S \leq \dot{P}_H H + P_H[F^d \varphi(\varepsilon) - (\alpha\delta H - E)].$$

But since the "poor" landlord is aware that credit financing is the relative expensive alternative he will lay claim on this margin as little as possible. The loan he raises in a given period in order to cover his investment expenses is instead

$$\text{(III.147)} \quad S = F^d \varepsilon + P_B F^d + zE.$$

---

*) From (III.142) it follows $\hat{P}_B = \beta\hat{\varepsilon}$, and (III.149) implies $\hat{P}_B = \hat{\varepsilon}$; moreover the growth equations for the housing stock and the stock of vacant land are still valid.

From equation (III.147) the following partial derivatives follow straightforwardly:

(III.148) $$\frac{\partial S}{\partial E} = z,$$

(III.149) $$\frac{\partial S}{\partial \varepsilon} = F^{d},$$

(III.150) $$\frac{\partial S}{\partial F^{d}} = \varepsilon + P_{B}$$

(III.151) $$\frac{\partial S}{\partial H} = 0.$$

Because the case considered now implies $\gamma_2 = 0$, it follows from (III.136) and (III.137) that

(III.152) $$\frac{\partial \mathcal{H}}{\partial S} = - \frac{\tau_I}{1-\tau_I} .$$

Using the general conditions (II.24), (II.28) - (II.30) and considering the partial derivatives in (III.148) - (III.151), the poor landlord's investment decisions have to fulfill the following conditions:

(III.153) $$P_H \left\{\begin{matrix} < \\ = \\ > \end{matrix}\right\} \frac{z}{1-\tau_I} \Rightarrow E \left\{\begin{matrix} = 0 \\ \geq 0, \\ = \alpha\delta H \end{matrix}\right. \qquad \text{for } t \geq t_o,$$

(III.154) $$P_H \varphi'(\varepsilon) = \frac{1}{1-\tau_I} \qquad \text{for } t \geq t^*,$$

(III.155) $$\frac{\beta}{\alpha}\varepsilon \left\{\begin{matrix} < \\ = \\ > \end{matrix}\right\} P_B \Rightarrow F^d \left\{\begin{matrix} = \\ \geq \end{matrix}\right\} 0 \qquad \text{for } t \geq t^*,$$

(III.156a) $$\hat{P}_H = 0 \qquad \text{for } t_o \leq t < t^*,$$

(III.156b) $$\hat{P}_H = - \frac{m}{P_H} + (1-\tau_I)r + \alpha\delta. \qquad \text{for } t \geq t^*.$$

Conditions (III.153) - (III.156b) confirm the conjecture that the "poor" landlord cannot enjoy the benefits of the income tax exemption of his imputed rental income to the same extent as his "wealthy" counterpart. Condition (III.156b) indicates that the user cost of capital decreases by the same relative amount as in the case of the "wealthy" owner-occupier or in the case where interest payments are tax deductible. In so far his equity tied in housing stock, i.e. accumulated capital gains, is as profitable as in the previously discussed cases. But the effective investment costs increase due to the non-deductibility of interest payments. This is shown by conditions (III.153) - (III.155). Because the landlord is forced to finance his investment with relatively expensive credits, maintenance investment is a rational option only if the house price exceeds the, compared to the tax free situation, higher level $1/(1-\tau_I)$. For the same reason the landlord will cut back his construction activities in the planning period. Since the income tax regulations discussed in this section do not discriminate against either one of the two factors of production (and thus do not affect the capital intensity, ε), condition (III.154) can only be fulfilled if in the new after-tax equilibrium the house price exceeds its laissez-faire level. This in turn implies that the optimal housing stock has to be lower than in the tax-free model.

Since these two opposing effects cannot be quantified without further information, the net impact of the tax exemption of imputed rental income on the "poor" owner-occupier's investment behaviour is ambigeous. However, we can conclude from the interdependence of the financing and investment decisions that it is always easier for the "wealthy" owner-occupier to acquire housing property. It is also worth noting that the results derived above do not allow for a similarly clear-cut general statement concerning the comparison between owner-occupying landlord and renting landlord. Which "type" of housing investor benefits more (suffers less) from income taxation cannot be settled without an appeal to specific data.

c) Owner-Occupation and the tax-exemption of realized capital gains

The analysis in sub-sections a) and b) assumed that, once acquired, the landlord utilizes his housing property until the end of its life. If the landlord's opportunity to sell his property is taken into account, it can be shown that it is more likely that present income tax laws might prefer the owner-occupier at least as far as liquidity aspects are concerned. Responsible for this result is the tax treatment of capital gains realized in the housing stock, H. In most countries of Western Europe the owner-occupier's realized capital gains are tax exempt, provided that a certain period of time between acquisition and sale has elapsed. In Canada, the owner-occupier's realized capital gains are subject to taxation to the extent that they exceed a well defined lifetime limit. The tax exempt amount is high enough to justify the judgment that in Canada also, capital gains from owner-occupation can be realized tax-free. The United States allows for the roll-over of realized capital gains (as far as owner occupation is concerned) contingent to the requirement that the seller within a well-defined time span purchases a home not cheaper than the one sold. Capital gains realized in rented housing stock, however, are generally subject to income taxation. Obviously, neither the U.S. regulations concerning owner-occupation nor the tax treatment of realized capital gains from rental accomodation bear a distinct advantage. Compared to this, the owner-occupier experiences an unambigeously preferential treatment in Canada as well as in Europe, whenever he decides to sell his home.

d) Towards an efficient taxation of housing income

It was mentioned earlier that none of the tax instruments currently applied to housing income satisfies the requirements of an efficient income taxation.

Causes for associated welfare losses are

- in the case of rental accomodation:
  - the present treatment of capital gains and capital losses in the stock of housing units,
  - the deductions for "depreciation" conceded by actual tax laws, and

- the immediate deductibility of maintenance expenditures;
- in the case of owner-occupation:
  - the tax exemption of the landlord's imputed rental income, and
  - the non-deductibility of interest-payments related to housing property.

The first step towards a more efficient taxation of housing income might be the abolition of the co-existence of two principally different taxation procedures. In the partial equilibrium context of our analysis the final goal would require

- the non-deductibility of maintenance expenditures and "depreciation" allowances and the consideration of changes in the market value of the housing stock over time;
- in the case of owner-occupation the taxation of the imputed rental income estimated according to the techniques introduced in subsection b).

However, there are two arguments that can be advanced against these proposals:

- from an administrative point of view it might be argued that the required regular assessment of housing property is too costly. If this objection is legitimate, the tax-exemption of accrued capital gains could be defended even because of welfare considerations;
- faced with the theoretical background of our analysis more momentous is the argument that the neutrality results derived in the preceding sections do not allow for judgments concerning the intertemporal efficiency of income taxation.

As a matter of fact it can be shown that the present treatment of imputed rental income from owner-occupation violates the conditions for an intersectoral efficient allocation of resources but may meet the requirements of intertemporal efficiency.

As is known from standard microeconomic analysis*) the intertemporal exchange optimum in a tax-free world can be characterized by the equality of the household's rate of time preference, π, and the rate of return on the economy's accumulated capital stock. In terms of our analysis this optimum can be described by condition

*) See, for example, Fisher (1931), or Hirshleifer (1970).

$$\text{(III.157)} \quad \pi(=r) = \frac{m}{P_H} + \hat{P}_H - \alpha\delta.$$

The comprehensive income tax described above is neutral in an intra-sectoral context - the after-tax situation still is characterized by

$$\text{(III.158)} \quad r = \frac{m}{P_H} + \hat{P}_H - \alpha\delta;$$

but because interest income is subject to taxation, the tax drives a wedge between the rate of time preference and the gross market interest rate:

$$\text{(III.159)} \quad \pi = (1-\tau_I)r.$$

Since the tax reduces the opportunity cost of dissaving, households are encouraged to increase their current consumption to the debit of future consumption, i.e. capital accumulation. The equilibrium after the imposition of the tax adjusts such that the rate of time preference is equal to the net market interest rate.

This tax-induced intertemporal distortion can be eliminated as far as owner-occupied housing is concerned, if imputed rental income is tax exempt and interest payments are tax deductible. In this case independent from the landlord's financial potential the tax has an impact only on the user cost of capital. It is

$$\text{(III.160)} \quad (1-\tau_I)r = \frac{m}{P_H} + \hat{P}_H - \alpha\delta.$$

Combining conditions (III.159) and (III.160) the equality of rate of time preference and rate of return can be shown. Since it is impossible to derive quantitative results from our analysis it is also impossible to say whether the inclusion of imputed rent in the income tax base is socially desirable or not.

The intra-sectoral inefficiency of the tax exemption of imputed rental income could be reduced if a taxation method could be formulated which increases the rentability of investment in rental accomodation to the same extent that the rentability of investment in owner-occupied housing rises due to taxation.

In recent years there has been considerable interest in constructing adequate tax systems which can avoid the intertemporal inefficiencies incurred by the present income tax laws. The proposals reach from a comprehensive expenditure tax to a taxation of the investor's "cash flow", whereby the taxable "cash flow" may be defined as the surplus resulting from real transactions [Brown (1948), Musgrave (1959), Smith (1963), Kay and King (1978)], as the profits distributed to the owner(s) of the firm [Meade Committee (1978)] or a combination of both [Sinn (1985)]. Obviously the imposition of an expenditure tax would require a principal reform of present tax systems. And as shown by Sinn, the realization of cash-flow systems à la Kay/King or Meade would imply the exclusion of a major income source from taxation, the interest income of households.

While Sinn's proposal yields the same results as the two other "cash-flow" systems, it does not require excessive amendments of current income tax laws. The only substantial change would provide the immediate deductibility of the gross investment cost. In turn, periodical depreciation allowances would have to be repealed.

Following Sinn's proposal, the appropriate description of the landlord's income tax liabilities is

$$\text{(III.160)} \quad T_l = \tau_I (mH - rD - F^d \varepsilon - P_B F^d - E)$$

Considering equation (III.160) the Hamiltonian corresponding to the landlord's decision problem reads

$$\text{(III.161)} \quad = (1-\tau_I)(zmH - zrD - F^d \varepsilon - P_B F^d - zE) + S$$

$$+ P_H [F^d \varphi(\varepsilon) - z(\alpha\delta H - E)]$$

$$+ \lambda_D S.$$

Because interest payments are tax deductible, the landlord will still be indifferent between the financing alternatives open to him. This can be proven by differentiating (III.161) with respect to S, considering $\lambda_D = -1$. The necessary conditions for optimal maintenance and construction are

$$\text{(III.162)} \quad P_H \left\{\begin{matrix} > \\ < \end{matrix}\right\} z(1-\tau_I) \Rightarrow E \begin{cases} = \alpha\delta H \\ \geq 0 \\ = 0 \end{cases} \qquad \text{for } t \geq t_o,$$

$$\text{(III.163)} \quad P_H \varphi'(\varepsilon) = (1-\tau_I) \qquad \text{for } t \geq t_o,$$

$$\text{(III.164)} \quad \frac{\beta}{\alpha}\varepsilon \left\{\begin{matrix} < \\ = \end{matrix}\right\} P_B \Rightarrow F^d \left\{\begin{matrix} = \\ \geq \end{matrix}\right\} 0 \qquad \text{for } t \geq t_o,$$

$$\text{(III.165a)} \quad \hat{P}_H = 0 \qquad \text{for } t_o \leq t < t^*,$$

$$\text{(III.165b)} \quad \hat{P}_H = - \frac{(1-\tau_I)m}{P_H} + (1-\tau_I)r + \alpha\delta \qquad \text{for } t \geq t^*.$$

Because of the immediate deductibility of gross investment costs, maintenance and investment in new housing both become more attractive. This is stated by conditions (III.162) - (III.164). That the tax regulations described above also have an influence on the user cost of capital in the sector of rental accomodation can be read from condition (III.165). But the same condition also states that this influence is ambigeous, depending on the relative size of the monetary rate of return, m/P_H, and the interest rate, r.

Despite this ambiguity it can be shown that over all the immediate deductibility of maintenance and new investment expenditures results in an unambigeously preferential treatment of housing investment, compared to the case of a comprehensive income tax. In order to do this, we define a houseprice $\overline{P}_H$ such that

$$\text{(III.166)} \quad \overline{P}_H = \frac{1}{1-\tau_I} P_H .$$

Substituting (III.166) into optimality conditions (III.162) - (III.165b) we obtain

$$(\text{III.162})' \quad \bar{P}_H \left\{\begin{matrix} > \\ < \end{matrix}\right\} z \Rightarrow E \begin{cases} = \alpha\delta H \\ = 0 \\ = 0 \end{cases}, \qquad \text{for } t \geq t_o,$$

$$(\text{III.163})' \quad \bar{P}_H \varphi'(\varepsilon) = 1, \qquad \text{for } t \geq t_o,$$

$$(\text{III.164})' \quad \frac{\beta}{\alpha}\varepsilon \left\{\begin{matrix} < \\ = \end{matrix}\right\} P_B \Rightarrow F^d \left\{\begin{matrix} = \\ \geq \end{matrix}\right\} 0, \qquad \text{for } t \geq t_o,$$

$$(\text{III.165a})' \quad \hat{\bar{P}}_H = 0 \qquad \text{for } t_o \leq t < t^*,$$

$$(\text{III.165b})' \quad \hat{\bar{P}}_H = -\frac{m}{\bar{P}_H} + (1-\tau_I)r + \alpha\delta. \qquad \text{for } t \geq t^*.$$

Obviously the tax on balance has an influence only on the user cost of capital - the user cost decrease in proportion to the income tax rate, τ_I. Combining condition (III.165b)' with the necessary condition for an intertemporal household equilibrium (III.159) confirms the desired equality between the rate of time preference and the net return on savings invested in the housing sector

$$(\text{III.167}) \quad \pi = (1-\tau_I)r = \hat{\bar{P}}_H + \frac{m}{\bar{P}_H} - \alpha\delta.$$

But not only that the immediate deduction of all investment costs is desirable under intertemporal considerations, it also presents some administrative advantages. The tax authorities do not have to keep track of the history of every single building and there is no need for a regular and costly assessment of housing property.

Authors Index

Subject Index

References

Aaron, H. (1970). "Income Taxes and Housing", **American Economic Review** 60, pp. 789.

Arcelus, F. and A.H. Meltzer (1973). "The Market for Housing and Housing Services", **Journal of Money, Credit and Banking** 5, pp. 78.

Arnott, R.J., and F.D. Lewis, (1979). "The Transition of Land to Urban Use", **J.P.E.** 87, pp. 161.

Arrow, K.J. (1951). "An Extension of the Basic Theorems of Classical Welfare Economics", in: J. Neymann (ed.), **Proceedings of the Second Berkeley Symposium on Mathematical Statistics on Probability,** Berkeley and Los Angeles.

Arrow, K.J. and M. Kurz (1970). **Public Investment and Optimal Fiscal Policy,** Baltimore.

Atkinson, A.B. (1977). "Housing Allowances, Income Maintenance and Income Taxation", in: The International Economic Association (ed.), **The Economics of Public Services,** Proceedings of a Conference held by the I.E.A. at Turin, pp. 3.

Auerbach, A.J. (1979). "Wealth Maximization and the Cost of Capital", **Quarterly Journal of Economics** 93, pp. 433.

_______________ (1981). "Inflation and the Tax Treatment of Firm Behaviour, **American Economic Review (Papers and Proceedings)** 71, pp. 419.

_______________ (1982). "Tax Neutrality and the Social Discount Rate", **Journal of Public Economics** 17, pp. 355.

Bailey, M.J. (1959). "Formal Criteria for Investment Decisions," **Journal of Political Economy** 67, pp. 476.

_______________ (1969). "Capital Gains and Income Taxation", in: A.C. Harberger and M.J. Bailey, (eds.), **The Taxation of Income from Capital,** Wahington, D.C., pp. 11.

Barro, R.J. (1974). "Are Government Bonds Net Wealth", **Journal of Political Economy,** pp. 1095.

Berck, P. (1979). "Open Access and Extinction", **Econometrica** 47, pp. 877.

Bergstrom, T.C. (1982). "On Capturing Oil Rents with a National Excise Tax", **American Economic Review** 72, pp. 194.

Boadway, R.W. (1978). "Investment Incentives, Corporate Taxation, and the Efficiency in the Allocation of Capital", **The Economic Journal** 88, pp. 470.

Boadway, R.W. (1979), **Public Sector Economics,** Cambridge (Mass.).

_______________, and H.M. Kitchen, (1984). **Canadian Tax Policy,** Toronto.

_______________, and N. Bruce (1984). **Welfare Economics,** Oxford.

Böhm-Bawerk, E.v. (1921). **Kredit und Kapitalzins, Teil II: Positive Theorie des Kapitals,** Band 1 (4. Auflage), Jena.

Boskin, M.J. (1978). "Taxation, Saving and the Rate of Interest", **Journal of Political Economy** 86, pp. 3.

Bourne, L.S. and J.R. Hitchcock (1978). **Urban Housing Markets.** Recent Directions on Research and Policy, Toronto.

Bradford, D. (1980). "Tax Neutrality and the Investment Tax Credit", in: H. Aaron and M. Boskin (eds.), **The Economics of Taxation,** pp. 281, Washington.

_______________ (1981). "The Incidence and Allocation Effects of a Tax on Corporate Distributions", **Journal of Public Economics** 15, pp. 1.

Brown, C. (1959). "Business Income Taxation and Investment Incentives", in: R. Musgrave and C. Shoup (eds.), **Readings in the Economics of Taxation,** London

Brueckner, J.K., B. von Rabenau, (1981). "Dynamics of Land Use for a Closed City", **Regional Science and Urban Economics,** pp. 1.

Buckley, R., R. Tuccillo and M. Villany (1977). **Capital Markets and the Housing Sector,** Cambridge (Mass.).

Burns, L. and L. Grebler (1977). **The Housing of Nations,** London.

Calvo, G.A., L.A. Kotlikoff, D.A. Rodriguez, (1979). "The Incidence of a Tax on Pure Rent: A New (?) Reason for an Old Answer", **Journal of Political Economy** 87, pp. 869.

Canada, (1966). **Report of the Royal Commission on Taxation,** Ottawa.

Charles, S. (1977). **Housing Economics,** London, Basinstoke.

Coase, R. (1937). "The Nature of the Firm", **Economica** 4, pp. 386.

Constantinides, G.M. and H. Scholes (1981). "Optimal liquidation of assets in the presence of personal tax: Implications for asset pricing", **Journal of Finance,** Papers and Proceedings.

Cordes, J. and S. Sheffrin (1981). "Taxation and the Sectoral Allocation of Capital in the U.S.", **National Tax Journal** 34, pp. 419.

Dasgupta, D.S. (1982). **The Control of Resource,** Cambridge, (Mass.).

__________ and G. Heal (1974). "Optimal Depletion and Exhaustible Resources", **Review of Economic Studies,** symposium, pp. 3.

_____________, __________, and J.E. Stiglitz (1980). **"The Taxation of Exhaustible Resources"**, Cambridge, England.

David, M. (1968). **Alternative Approaches to Capital Gains Taxation,** Washington, D.C..

De Leeuw, F. (1971). "The Demand for Housing; a Review of Cross-Section Evidence", **Review of Economic Studies** 53.

Diewert, W. (1974). "Intertemporal Consumer Theory and the Demand for Durables", **Econometrica** 42, pp. 497.

Dorfmann, R., P. Samuelson and R. Solow (1958), **Linear Programming and Economic Analysis,** New York, Toronto, London.

Downs, A. (1973). **Federal Housing Subsidies: How Are They Working?** Toronto, London.

Ebnet, O. (1978). **Die Besteuerung des Wertzuwachses. Ein theoretischer Ansatz im Rahmen der Einkommensbesteuerung,** Baden-Baden.

Engels. F. (1923). **Anti-Dühring,** 12. Auflage, Berlin.

Fair, R. (1972). "Disequilibrium in Housing Models", **Journal of Finance** 27, pp. 207.

Feldstein, M. (1974). "Incidence of a Capital Income Tax in a Growing Economy With Variable Saving Rates", **Review of Economic Studies** 41, pp. 505.

______________ (1977). "The Surprising Incidence of a Tax on Pure Rent: A New Answer to an Old Question", **Journal of Political Economy** 85, pp. 349.

______________ (1978). "The Welfare Cost of Capital Income Taxation", **Journal of Political Economy** 86, pp. 29.

______________ and Yitzhaki, S., (1978). "The Effects of the Capital Gains Tax on the Selling and Switching of Common Stock", **Journal of Public Economics** 9, pp. 17.

Fisher, I. (1907). **The Rate of Interest. It's Nature, Determination and Relation to Economic Phenomena,** New York.

Fisher, I. (1931). **The Theory of Interest Rates as Determined by Impatience to Spend Income and Opportunity to Invest it,** New York.

Friauf, K., W. Risse and K.P. Winters (1978). **Der Beitrag steuerlicher Maßnahmen zur Lösung der Bodenfrage,** Schriftenreihe "Städtebauliche Forschung" des Bundesministeriums für Raumordnung, Bauwesen und Städteplanung, Bad Godesberg.

Fujita, M. (1982). "Spatial Patterns of Residential Development", **Journal of Urban Economics** 12, pp. 22.

Gschwendtner, H. (1975). "Wirkung der Bodenwertzuwachssteuer auf Bodenpreise und Bodenspekulation", **Jahrbücher für Nationalökonomie und Statistik**, pp. 29.

Haig, R. (1921). "The Concept of Income - Economic and Legal Aspects", in: R. Haig et al. (eds.), **The Federal Income Tax**, New York.

Hall, R. and D. Jorgenson (1967). "Tax Policy and Investment Behaviour", **American Economic Review** 57, pp. 391.

Haller, H. (1973). "Grundsätzliches zur Besteuerung von Grundstücksgewinnen", **Kredit und Kapital** 6, pp. 255.

Halliwell, J. (1969). "The Taxation of Capital Gains", **Canadian Journal of Economics** 2, pp. 314.

Harberger, A. (1962). "The Incidence of the Corporation Income Tax", **Journal of Political Economy** 70, pp. 215.

Hartwick, J.M. and N.D. Olewiler (1986). The Economics of Natural Resource Use, Cambridge.

Hellwig, M. (1981). "Bankruptcy, Limited Liability and the Modigliani-Miller Theorem", **American Economic Review** 71, pp. 155.

Hendershott, P. (1980). "Real User Cost and the Demand for Single-Family Housing", **Brooking Papers on Economic Activity**, pp. 402.

Hendershott, P. and J. Slemrod (1982). **Taxes and the User Cost of Capital for Owner-Occupied Housing**, National Bureau of Economic Research, Cambridge (Mass.).

Henderson, J. and Y. Ioannides (1983). "A Model of Housing Tenure Choice", **American Economic Review** 73, pp. 98.

Hirshleifer (1970). **Investment, Interest and Capital**, Englewood Cliffs.

Hotelling, H. (1931). "The Economics of Exhaustible Resources", **Journal of Political Economy** 39, pp. 137.

Hughes, G. (1980). "Housing and the Tax System", in: G. Hughes and G. Heal (eds.), **Public Policy and the Tax System**, London.

Intrilligator, M.D. (1971). **Mathematical Optimization and Economic Theory**, Englewood Cliffs.

Jaffee, D. (1972). "An Econometric Model of the Mortgage Market", in: M. Gramlich and D. Jaffee (eds.), **Savings, Deposits, Mortgages and Residential Construction**, Lexington.

Jatzek, H. and W. Leibfritz (1982). **Der Einfluß der Steuern auf die Investitionstätigkeit der Unternehmen**, Berlin und München.

Johansson, S.E. (1961). **Skatt - Investering - Värdering,** Stockholm.

Jorgenson, D. (1963). "Capital Theory and Investment Behaviour", **American Economic Review (Papers and Proceedings)** 53, pp. 247.

______________ (1967). "The Theory of Investment Behaviour, in: R. Ferber (ed.), **Determinants of Investment Behaviour,** New York.

Kamien, M.I., Schwatz, N.C. (1981). **Dynamic Optimization,** New York and Oxford.

Kanemoto, Y. (1985). "Housing as an Asset and the Effects of Property Taxation on the Residential Development Process", **Journal of Urban Economic** 15, pp. 145.

Kay, J. and M. King (1978). **The British Tax System,** Oxford.

Kemp, M.C. and N. van Long (1980). **Exhaustible Resources, Optimality and Trade,** Amsterdam.

Kiefer, D. (1981). "The Interaction of Inflation and the U.S. Tax Subsidies on Housing", **National Tax Journal** 34, pp. 433.

King, A. (1977). "The Demand for Housing", **Southern Economic Journal** 43, pp. 1077.

Kovenock, D.J. and M. Rothschild (1982). "Capital Gains Taxation in an Economy with an Austrian Sector", **Journal of Public Economics** 21, pp. 215.

Laidler, D. (1969). "Income Tax Incentives for Owner-Occupied Housing", in: A. Harberger and M. Bailey (eds.), **The Taxation of Income from Capital,** Washington.

Lange, O. (1944). "The Foundations of Welfare Economics, **Econometrica** 10, pp. 215.

Lange, O. and F. Taylor (1948). **On the Economic Theory of Socialism,** 2nd edition, Minneapolis.

Lee, T. (1968). "Housing and Permanent Income", **Review of Economic Studies** 50.

Litzenberger, R. and H. Sosin (1978). "Taxation and the Incidence of Homeownership Across Income Groups", **Journal of Finance** 33, pp. 947.

Maisel, S. (1963). "A Theory of Fluctuations in Residential Construction Starts", **American Economic Review** 53, pp. 359.

Malinvaud, E. (1953). "Capital Accumulation and Efficient Allocation of Resources", **Econometrica** 21, pp. 233.

______________ (1962). "Efficient Capital Accumulation - Corrigendum", **Econometrica** 30, pp. 570.

Markusen, J.R. and D.T. Scheffmann (1978). "The Timing of Residential Land Development: A General Equilibrium Approach", **Journal of Urban Economics** 8, pp. 411.

Mayo, S. (1981). "Theory and Estimation in the Economics of Housing Demand" **Journal of Urban Economics** 10, pp. 95.

Meade-Committee (1978). **The Structure and Reform of Direct Taxation.** Report of a Committee chaired by Prof. J. Meade, London, Boston, Sidney.

Meltzer, A. (1974). "Credit Availability and Economic Decisions", **Journal of Finance** 29, pp. 263.

Miller, M. (1977). "Debt and Taxes", **Journal of Finance** 32, pp. 261.

_______________ and F. Modigliani (1958). "The Cost of Capital, Corporation Finance and the Theory of Investment", **American Economic Review** 48, pp. 259.

Mohring, H. (1961). "Land Values and the Measurement of Highway Benefits", **Journal of Political Economy** 69, pp. 236.

Möller, H. (1967). **Der Boden in der Politischen Ökonomie**, Wiesbaden.

Moorhouse, J.C. (1972). "Optimal Housing Maintenance under Rent Control", **Southern Economic Journal** 34, pp. 93.

Musgrave, R.A. (1959). **The Theory of Public Finance**, New York, Toronto, etc.

Muth, R. (1960). "The Demand for Non-Farming Housing", in: A. Harberger (ed.), **The Demand for Durable Goods**, Chicago.

Nachtkamp, H.H. (1984). "Das Für und Wider staatlicher Interventionen in den Wohnungsbau und die Wohnversorgung", in: H. Siebert (ed.), **Intertemporale Allokation**, Frankfurt.

Nell-Breuning, O.v. (1956). "Erfassung der steigenden Grundrente", **Wirtschaft und Gesellschaft**, Band I, Freiburg.

Olsen, E. (1969). "A Competitive Theory of the Housing Market", **American Economic Review** 59, pp. 612.

_______________ (1971). "Subsidized Housing in a Competitive Market", **American Economic Review** 61, pp. 220.

Page, T. (1977). **Conservation and Economic Efficiency.** An Approach to Materials Policy, Baltimore.

Pines, D., E. Werczberger (1982). "A Linear Programming Model of the Urban Housing Markets: Static and Dynamic Aspects", **Regional Science and Urban Economics** 12, pp. 211.

Pindyck, R.S. (1978). "The Optimal Exploration and Production of Non-Renewable Resources", **Journal of Political Economy** 86, pp. 841.

Rabenau, B.v. (1973). **Urban Dynamic Models**, Ph.D. Dissertation, Berkely.

Ricardo, D. (1951). "On the Principles of Political Economy and Taxation", edited by R. Sraffa, New York.

Robinson, R. (1979). **Housing Economics and Public Policy**, London.

Rolph, E. (1983). "Discriminating Effects of the Income Tax Treatment of Owner-Occupants", **National Tax Journal** 36, pp. 471.

Sandmo, A. and A. Atkinson (1980). "Welfare Implications of the Taxation of Savings", **Economic Journal** 90, pp. 529.

Schanz, G. (1886). "Der Einkommensbegriff und die Einkommensteuergesetze", **Finanzarchiv** 13, pp. 1.

Schneider, D. (1974). **Investition und Finanzierung.** Lehrbuch der Investitions-, Finanzierungs- und Ungewißheitstheorie, Opladen.

Shelton, J.P. (1968). "The Cost of Renting Versus Owning a Home", **Land Economics** 14, pp. 59.

Shoup, C. (1970). "The White Paper: Accrual Accounting for Capital Gains and Losses", **Canadian Tax Journal** 18, pp. 96.

Simons, H.C. (1938). **Personal Income Taxation**, Chicago and London.

Sinn, H.W. (1985a). "The Problem of Vacant Land", discussion paper, University of Western Ontario, forthcoming in: Regional Science and Urban Economics.

______________(1985b). Kapitaleinkommensbesteuerung, Tübingen.

Smith, B. (1976). "The Supply of Urban Housing", **Quarterly Journal of Economics** 90.

Stiglitz, J.E. (1974). "Growth with Exhaustible Natural Resources: Efficient and Optimal Growth Paths" **Review of Economic Studies**, Symposium, pp. 123.

______________ (1981). "Pareto-Optimality and Competition", **Journal of Finance** 36, pp. 235.

______________ (1983). "Some Aspects of the Taxation of Capital Gains", **Journal of Public Economics** 21, pp. 257.

Timm, H. (1980). "Steuervergünstigungen und Transferzahlungen als Instrumente der staatlichen Allokations- und Stabilitätspolitik - ein kritischer Vergleich", in: H. Siebert (ed.) **Politik und Markt**, Stuttgart und New York.

Tullock, G. (1971). "Subsidized Housing in a Competitive Market; Comment", **American Economic Review** 61, pp. 218.

Vandell, K. (1982). "Towards a Model of Credit Rationing and Term Adjustment in the Mortgage Market", in: C. Sirmans (ed.), **Research in Real Estate** 1, Toronto.

Vosgerau, H.J. (1972). "Boden und wirtschaftliches Wachstum", **Kyklos**, pp. 481.

Wasserfallen, W. (1979). "Wohnungsmarkt und Kreditmärkte", **Schweizerische Zeitschrift für Volkswirtschaft und Statistik**, pp. 139.

Weiss, J. (1978). "Capital Gains, Discriminatory Taxes and the Choice Between Renting and Owning a House", **Journal of Public Economics** 10, pp. 45.

White, M. and L. White (1977). "The Tax Subsidy to Owner-Occupied Housing: Who Benefits?", **Journal of Public Economics** 7, pp. 111.

MIX
Papier aus verantwortungsvollen Quellen
Paper from responsible sources
FSC® C105338

If you have any concerns about our products,
you can contact us on
ProductSafety@springernature.com

In case Publisher is established outside the EU,
the EU authorized representative is:
Springer Nature Customer Service Center GmbH
Europaplatz 3, 69115 Heidelberg, Germany

Printed by Libri Plureos GmbH
in Hamburg, Germany